EASY ITALIAN PHRASE BOOK

Over 1500 Common Phrases For Everyday Use And Travel

Lingo Mastery

www.LingoMastery.com

ISBN-13: 978-1-951949-06-8

Free Book Reveals The 6 Step Blueprint That Took Students
<u>From Language Learners To Fluent In 3 Months</u>

- **6 Unbelievable Hacks** that will accelerate your learning curve
- **Mind Training:** why memorizing vocabulary is easy
- **One Hack To Rule Them All:** This <u>secret nugget</u> will blow you away...

Head over to **<u>LingoMastery.com/hacks</u>**
and claim your free book now!

CONTENTS

Introduction 1

Colors...9

Numbers 14

Greetings..18

Date and Time 25

Common Questions 30

When Someone Is Being Rude.................40

Medical 44

Ordering Food 53

Transportation...69

Religious Questions..................................80

Emergency 83

Technology...87

Conversation Tips 95

Date Night..98

Money and Shopping.............................107

Children and Pets..................................119

Traveler's Guide.....................................127

Answers 129

Directions...135

Apologies 138

Small Talk 140

Business 147

The Weather 157

Hotel... 160

Sports and Exercise 167

The First 24 Hours After Arriving 175

The Last 24 Hours Before Leaving 177

More from Lingo Mastery... 180

Conclusion 186

INTRODUCTION

If you have finally decided to visit one of the most beautiful countries in the world, then you can't help but consider the words, phrases, ways of saying that you will use in certain situations, which you must know before leaving.

Thanks to this book, we will see how to deal with many situations that can be simple, complicated, funny or even not funny at all. All those real situations that a tourist will experience when, for example, they want to drink a coffee, order a good *amatriciana*, or simply tell the waiter that what they have just eaten has not been to their liking.

Think of the souvenirs to bring back to a relative. Do you want to negotiate on the price or ask for a discount? It is certainly here that you will need to find the way to express yourself correctly.

Most of the time, a translation with the vocabulary at your fingertips is the best solution and therefore, why not take precautions and study a few phrases that could amaze your fellow travelers or your interlocutors?

Of course, there are some obstacles to overcome. Let's see for example what can create difficulties at a phonetic level in the Italian language.

How to pronounce the Italian vowels

There are five vowels in the Italian language: A, E, I, O, U.

Every vowel, depending on its surrounding letters, can either be short or long.

A vowel is long when it is stressed and there are no consonant clusters following it. Eg.

Fato
Fate

A vowel is short when it is stressed and it's followed by a consonant cluster, and at the end of a word.

Fatto

Done

The "to" syllables in both words feature a short "o" vowel. Vowels that are not stressed are all short.

The vowel A

The Italian "a" sound resembles the "a" in father, but it's wider. You must pronounce it only in this way. There's only one way you can pronounce this sound (always remember the distinction between short and long vowels).

Allegria

Cheerfulness

Onestà

Honesty

It's rare for an Italian vowel to be stressed at the end of a word, and when it is it is marked with an accent, as in onestà here.

The vowel E

"E" has two pronunciations, a narrow and a wide pronunciation.

Elemento

Element

Perché

Why/because

Palestra

Gym

È

(It) is

The first two words feature a close "e", while the "e" in palestra is wide. As in velocità, perché is stressed on the last syllable so it carries a mark. È is a conjugation of the verb essere, to be, and it carries a mark so that it is distinguishable from e, the Italian translation of and, which in standard Italian is pronounced with a close sound.

At the end of a word, é is pronounced close.

The vowel I

Intero
Whole/Entire
Colibrì
Hummingbird

The vowel O

Orso
Bear
Otre
Wineskin
Farò
I will do

Final ò sounds are always open, like the o in occhi. You'll hear the two o's in orto have a different sound. Notice that if you miss the accent mark on the last word, farò, you will write faro, which is pronounced very differently (the stress will be on the "a" vowel and not on the last syllable) and it will mean lighthouse!

Faro
Lighthouse

The vowel U

Uva
Grapes
Cucù
Cuckoo

Pronunciation of vowels combination

Every vowel in a vowel combination, in the Italian language is pronounced. Following here the possible combination.

The vowel combination AA

AA, as a long "a" in "father"
Affettato

The vowel combination AE

AE, ah eh

Paese

The vowel combination AI

AI, pronounced as "eye"

Airone

The vowel combination AO

AO, ah oh

Ciao

The vowel combination AU

AU, ah ooh

Audizione

The vowel combination EA

EA, eh ah

Platea

The vowel combination EE

EE, pronounced as a long "eh" sound

Dee

The vowel combination EI

EI, eh ee

Veicolo

The vowel combination EO

EO, eh oh

Meteo

The vowel combination EU

EU, eh oo

Europa

The vowel combination IA

IA, ee ah
Malattia

The vowel combination IE

IE, ee eh
Piene

The vowel combination II

II, a long "ee" sound
Sii

The vowel combination IO

IO, ee oh
Iodio

The vowel combination IU

IU, ee oo
Aiuto

The vowel combination OA

OA, oh ah
Oasi

The vowel combination OE

OE, oh eh
Poema

The vowel combination OI

OI, oh ee
Poi

The vowel combination OO

OO, oh oh
OU, oh oo, is found in loanwords from English and French, such as "outlet", and Italian words with this sound are pretty unique.
Zoo

The vowel combination UA

UA, oo ah
Tua

The vowel combination UE

UE, oo eh
Sue

The vowel combination UI

UI, oo ee
Suino

The vowel combination UO

UO, oo oh
Vuoto

The vowel combination UU

UU, oo oo
Perpetuum

How to pronounce the Italian consonants

Now that we've seen the Italian vowels, it's time to look at how consonants behave. Most consonants are pronounced as in English, however you have to be careful with a few of them.

Unlike the English consonants, the Italian consonants can also undergo what is called gemination in linguistics: double consonants, like TT, LL and MM, are audibly longer than T, L and M consonants alone.

Let's see the important consonants in detail.

The consonant C

C is never aspirated in Italian, and it means that it is never followed by a puff of air as in "cat".

When the consonant precedes -e or -i, C has a "ch" sound, like in "check". Otherwise, in front of -a, -o and -u it behaves like the English "k".

CIA, CIO, CIU are pronounced like cha, cho, choo respectively.

CH is pronounced like "k".

The consonant G

The consonant follows the same rules of C, so:

- In front of -e and -i it is pronounced like the "j" in "John"
- It has a hard "g" sound in front of -a, -o and -u, as in "guide"
- GIA, GIO and GIU are pronounced like jah, joh and joo
- GH behaves like the "g" in "game"

Pronouncing GL

This consonant cluster has a sound that doesn't exist in the English language, but the "lli" cluster in "million" is a good starting point.

Tip for you: raise your tongue towards the palate while pronouncing "L"

Pronouncing GN

It is pronounced like the Spanish ñ. Raise your tongue towards the palate while pronouncing "N" .

The consonant H

Unlike English, the Italian H at the beginning of a word is always silent. In other words, Hanno = they have, is pronounced an-no. However, the Italian H changes the pronunciation of some consonants such as G and C when it follows them, as already pointed out.

The consonant P

It's never aspirated. Beware of geminates!

The consonant Q

Like the English "k".

The consonant R

It's trilled, like the Spanish R, but it's not as long as the Spanish one.

Tip: the single "r" sound resembles the faint "d" sound that results from pronouncing "butter" or "water" with an American accent. See if you can roll the tip of your tongue starting with that sound!

The consonant S

In standard Italian, if between vowels or before a voiced consonant it's pronounced voiced, sounding exactly like the "s" in "case". This is unlike English, where words like "sleep" or "snake" are pronounced with an unvoiced S. In all other cases, it's pronounced like the "s" in "six".

Pronouncing SC

When it precedes -e and -i it's pronounced like the "sh" in "shake". In front of -a, -o and -u it sounds like the "sk" in "skate".

The consonant T

It's never aspirated!

The consonant Z

In standard Italian, it's voiced at the beginning of a word, unless the next syllable contains an unvoiced consonant, when it's between vowels, and it's unvoiced when it belongs to a verb ending in -izzare.

Where is the stress?

About 75% of the words are stressed on the second to last syllable, like "Portone", "Labirinto", "Nessuno".

When a word has an accent mark on the last vowel, the stress is always on that vowel:

Notice that if you miss the accent mark on "sospirò", you'll actually say something else, "sospiro", which can either mean "sigh" or "I sigh" depending on context! So accent marks are important.

Superlatives, that means adjectives ending in -issimo, -issima, -issimi and -issime, are stressed on the third to last syllable.

COLORS

Note: Please raise your tongue to your palate in order to pronounce the "GN" and "GL" sounds in all the words marked with an asterisk.

Gold	**Blue**	**Purple**
Oro	Blu	Viola
O-ro	*BLOO*	*vee-O-la*

Red	**Light blue**	**White**
Rosso	Azzurro	Bianco
ROS-so	*az-ZOOR-ro*	*bee-AN-ko*

Orange	**Violet**	**Black**
Arancione	Viola	Nero
a-ran-CHO-neh	*vee-O-la*	*NEH-ro*

Yellow	**Pink**	**Gray**
Giallo	Rosa	Grigio
JAL-lo	*RO-sa*	*GREE-jee-o*

Green	**Brown**	**Silver**
Verde	Marrone	Argento
VER-deh	*mar-RO-neh*	*ar-JEN-to*

What color is that sign?
Di che colore è quel cartello?
Dee keh ko-LO-reh eh KWEL kar-TEL-lo?

Is the cartoon in color?
Il cartone animato è a colori?
eel kar-TO-neh a-nee-MA-to eh a ko-LO-ree?

Is this television show in color?
Lo spettacolo televisivo è a colori?
lo spet-TA-ko-lo teh-leh-vee-SEE-vo eh ah ko-LO-ree?

This is a red pen.
Questa è una penna rossa.
KWES-ta eh OO-na PEN-na ROS-sa.

This piece of paper is blue.
Questo pezzo di carta è blu.
KWES-to PEZ-zo dee KAR-ta eh BLOO.

What color is that car?
Di che colore è quella macchina?
dee keh ko-LO-reh eh KWEL-la MAK-kee-na?

What color are your clothes?
Di che colore sono i tuoi vestiti?
dee keh ko-LO-reh SO-no ee too-O-ee ves-TEE-tee?

Is this the right color?
È questo il colore giusto?
eh KWES-to il ko-LO-reh JOOS-to?

What color is the stop light?
Di che colore è la luce che indica lo stop?
dee keh ko-LO-reh eh la LOO-cheh ke EEN-dee-ka lo stop?

Does that color mean danger?
Quel colore significa* pericolo?
KWEL ko-LO-reh see-NEE-fee-ka peh-REE-ko-lo?

That bird is red.
Quell'uccello è rosso.
KWEL oo-CHEL-lo eh ROS-so.

What color is that animal?
Di che colore è quell'animale?
dee keh ko-LO-reh eh kwel a-nee-MA-leh?

The sky is blue.
Il cielo è blu.
eel CHE-lo eh BLOO.

The clouds are white.
Le nuvole sono bianche.
leh NOO-vo-leh SO-no bee-AN-keh.

That paint is blue.
Quella vernice è blu.
KWEL-la ver-NEE-cheh eh BLOO.

Press the red button.
Premi il tasto rosso.
PREH-mee eel TA-sto ROS-so.

Don't press the red button.
Non premere il tasto rosso.
non PREH-meh-reh eel TA-sto ROS-so.

Black and White.
Bianco e nero.
bee-AN-ko eh NEH-ro.

Look at all the colors.
Guarda tutti i colori.
GWAR-da TOOT-tee ee ko-LO-ree

Is that a color television?
È una televisione a colori?
eh OO-na teh-leh-vee-see-O-neh ah ko-LO-ree?

What color do you see?
Che colore vedi?
KEH ko-LO-reh VEH-dee?

Can I have the color blue?
Posso avere il colore blu?
POS-so a-VEH-reh eel ko-LO-reh BLOO?

What color do you have for these frames?
Che colore usi per queste cornici?
KEH ko-LO-reh OO-see per KWES-teh kor-NEE-chee?

Don't go until the color is green.
Non partire fino a che il colore non diventa verde.
non par-TEE-reh FEE-no a keh eel ko-LO-reh non dee-VEN-ta.

Coloring pencils.
Matite colorate.
ma-TEE-teh ko-lo-RA-teh.

Coloring pens.
Pennarelli.
pen-na-REL-lee.

The sharpie is black.
Il pennarello è nero.
eel pen-na-REL-lo eh NE-ro.

I passed with flying colors.
Sono passato a pieni voti.
SO-no pas-SA-to a pee-EH-nee VO-tee.

Do you have this in another color?
Ce l'hai di un altro colore?
cheh LA-ee dee oon AL-tro ko-LO-reh?

Do you have this in a darker color?
Ce l'hai di un colore più scuro?
cheh LAH-ee dee oon ko-LO-reh PEW SKOO-ro?

Do you have this in a lighter color?
Ce l'hai di un colore più chiaro?
cheh LAH-ee dee oon ko-LO-reh PEW kee-A-ro?

Can you paint my house blue?
Puoi pitturarmi la casa di blu?
poo-O-ee pit-too-RAR-mee la KA-sa dee BLOO?

Can you paint my car the same color?
Puoi pitturarmi l'automobile dello stesso colore?
poo-O-ee pit-too-RAR-mee la-oo-to-MO-bee-leh DEL-lo STES-so ko-LO-reh?

The flag has three different colors.
La bandiera ha tre colori diversi.
la ban-dee-EH-ra a TREH ko-LO-ree dee-VER-see.

Is the color on the flag red?
Il colore sulla bandiera è rosso?
eel ko-LO-reh SOOL-la ban-dee-EH-ra eh ROS-so?

NUMBERS

Zero
Zero
ZEH-ro

One
Uno
OO-no

Two
Due
DOO-eh

Three
Tre
TREH

Four
Quattro
KWAT-tro

Five
Cinque
CHIN-kweh

Six
Sei
SEH-ee

Seven
Sette
SET-teh

Eight
Otto
OT-to

Nine
Nove
NO-veh

Ten
Dieci
dee-EH-chee

Eleven
Undici
OON-dee-chee

Twelve
Dodici
DO-dee-chee

Thirteen
Tredici
TREH-dee-chee

Fourteen
Quattordici
KWAT-tor-dee-chee

Fifteen
Quindici
KWIN-dee-chee

Sixteen
Sedici
SEH-dee-chee

Seventeen
Diciassette
dee-chas-SET-teh

Eighteen
Diciotto
dee-CHOT-to

Nineteen
Diciannove
dee-chan-NO-veh

Twenty
Venti
VEN-tee

Twenty-one
Ventuno
ven-TOO-no

Twenty-two
Ventidue
ven-tee-DOO-eh

Twenty-three
Ventitré
ven-tee-TREH

Twenty-four
Ventiquattro
ven-tee-KWAT-tro

Twenty-five
Venticinque
ven-tee-CHIN-kweh

Twenty-six
Ventisei
ven-tee-SEH-ee

Twenty-seven
Ventisette
ven-tee-SET-teh

Twenty-eighth
Ventotto
ven-TOT-to

Twenty-nine
Ventinove
ven-tee-NO-veh

Thirty
Trenta
TREN-ta

Forty
Quaranta
kwa-RAN-ta

Fifty
Cinquanta
chin-KWAN-ta

Sixty
Sessanta
ses-SAN-ta

Seventy
Settanta
set-TAHN-ta

Eighty
Ottanta
ot-TAN-ta

Ninety
Novanta
no-VAN-ta

One-hundred
Cento
CHEN-to

Two-hundred
Duecento
doo-eh-CHEN-to

Five-hundred
Cinquecento
chin-kweh-CHEN-to

One-thousand
Mille
MEEL-leh

One-hundred-thousand
Centomila
chen-to-MEE-la

One million
Un milione
oon mee-lee-O-neh

One billion
Un miliardo
oon mee-lee-AR-do

What does that add up to?
Che cosa si aggiunge?
ke KO-sa see aj-JOON-jeh?

What number is on this paper?
Che numero è scritto su questo foglio*?
ke NOO-meh-ro EH s-KREET-to soo KWES-to FOL-lee-o?

*NOTE: Raise your tongue towards the palate while pronouncing "L".

What number is on this sign?
Che numero è scritto su questo cartello?
ke NOO-meh-ro EH s-KREET-to soo KWES-to kar-TEL-lo?

Are these two numbers equal?
Questi due numeri sono uguali?
KWES-tee DOO-eh NOO-meh-ree SO-no oo-goo-A-lee?

My social security number is one, two, three, four, five.
Il mio numero di previdenza sociale è uno, due, tre, quattro, cinque.
eel MEE-o NOO-meh-ro DEE preh-vee-DEN-za so-chee-AH-leh eh OO-no, DOO-eh, TREH, KWAT-tro, CHIN-kweh.

I'm going to bet five-hundred Euros.
Ho intenzione di scommettere cinquecento euro.
o een-ten-zee-O-neh dee skom-MET-teh-reh chin-kweh-CHEN-to EH-oo-ro.

Can you count to one-hundred for me?
Puoi contare fino a cento per me?
POO-o-ee kon-TA-reh FEE-no a CHEN-to per MEH?

I took fourteen steps.
Ho fatto quattordici passi.
o FAT-to KWAT-tor-dee-chee PAS-see.

I ran two kilometers.
Ho corso per due chilometri.
oh KOR-so per DOO-eh kee-LO-meh-tree.

The speed limit is 30 km/h.
Il limite di velocità è di trenta chilometri orari.
eel LEE-mee-teh DEE veh-lo-chee-TA eh dee TREN-ta kee-LO-meh-tree O-ra-ree.

What are the measurements?
Quali sono le misure?
KWA-lee SO-no leh mee-SOO-reh?

Can you dial this number?
Puoi comporre questo numero?
POO-o-ee kom-POR-reh KWES-to NOO-meh-ro?

One dozen.
Una dozzina.
OO-na doz-ZEE-na.

A half dozen.
Mezza dozzina.
MEZ-za doz-ZEE-na.

How many digits are in the number?
Quante cifre ci sono nel numero?
KWAN-teh CHEE-freh chee SO-no nel NOO-meh-ro?

My phone number is nine, eight five, six, two, one, eight, seven, eight, eight.
Il mio numero di telefono è nove, otto, cinque, sei, due, uno, otto, sette, otto, otto.
eel MEE-o NOO-meh-ro dee teh-LEH-fo-no eh NO-veh, OT-to, CHIN-kweh, SEH-ee, DOO-eh, OO-no, OT-to, SET-teh, OT-to, OT-to.

The hotel's phone number is one eight-hundred, three, two three, five, seven, five, five.
Il numero di telefono dell'hotel è ottocento, tre, due, tre, cinque, sette, cinque, cinque.
eel NOO-meh-ro dee teh-LEH-fo-no dell-oh-TEL eh ot-to-CHEN-to, TREH, DOO-eh, TREH, CHIN-kweh, SET-teh, CHIN-kweh, CHIN-kweh.

The taxi number is six, eight, one, four, four, four, five, eight, one, nine.
Il numero del taxi è sei, otto, uno, quattro, quattro, quattro, cinque, otto, uno, nove.
eel NOO-meh-ro del taxi eh SEH-ee, OT-to, OO-no, KWAT-tro, CHIN-kweh, OT-to, OO-no, NO-veh.

Call my hotel at two, one, four, seven, one, two, nine, five, seven, six.
Chiama il mio hotel al due, uno, quattro, sette, uno, due, nove, cinque, sette, sei.
kee-A-ma eel MEE-o o-TEL al DOO-eh, OO-no, KWAT-tro, SET-teh, OO-no, DOO-eh, NO-veh, CHIN-kweh, SET-teh, SEH-ee.

Call the embassy at nine, eight, nine, eight, four, three, two, one, seven, one.
Chiama l'ambasciata al nove, otto, nove, otto, quattro, tre, due, uno, sette, uno.
kee-AH-ma lam-ba-shee-A-ta al NO-veh, OT-to, NO-veh, OT-to, KWAT-tro, TREH, DOO-eh, OO-no, SET-teh, OO-no.

GREETINGS

Hello!
Ciao!
chee-A-o!

How's it going?
Come stai?
KO-meh STA-ee?

What's new?
Hai delle novità?
a-EE DEL-leh no-vee-TA?

What's going on?
Che succede?
ke soo-CHEH-deh?

Home, sweet home.
Casa, dolce casa.
KA-sa DOL-cheh KA-sa.

Ladies and gentlemen, thank you for coming.
Signore* e signori*, grazie di essere venuti.
see-nee-O-reh eh see-nee-O-ree, GRA-zee-eh dee ES-seh-reh ve-NOO-tee.

*NOTE: Raise your tongue towards the palate while pronouncing "N"

How is everything?
Come vanno le cose?
KO-meh VAN-no leh KO-seh?

Long time no see.
Non ci si vede da parecchio.
non chee see VEH-deh da pa-REH-kee-o.

It's been a long time.
Ne è passato di tempo.
neh eh pas-SA-to dee TEM-po.

It's been a while!
È da un po' che non ci si vede!
eh da oon PO ke non chi see VEH-deh!

How is life?
Come va la vita?
KO-me VA la VEE-ta?

How is your day?
Come butta?
KO-me BOO-ta?

Good morning.
Buongiorno.
BOO-on jee-OR-no.

It's been too long!
È passato davvero troppo tempo!
eh pas-SA-to dav-VEH-ro TROP-po TEM-po!

Good afternoon.
Buon pomeriggio.
BOO-on po-meh-REEJ-jee-o.

How long has it been?
Quanto tempo è passato?
KWAN-to TEM-po eh pas-SA-to ?

It's a pleasure to meet you.
È un piacere conoscerti.
eh oon pee-a-CHEH-reh ko-NO-sher-tee.

It's always a pleasure to see you.
È sempre un piacere vederti.
eh SEM-preh oon pee-a-CHEH-reh veh-DER-tee.

Allow me to introduce Earl, my husband.
Permettimi di presentarti Earl, mio marito.
per-MET-tee-mee dee pre-sen-TAR-tee MEE-o ma-REE-to.

Goodnight.
Buonanotte.
boo-o-na-NOT-teh.

May I introduce my brother and sister?
Posso presentarti mio fratello e mia sorella?
POS-so pre-sen-TAR-tee a MEE-a so-REL-la?

Good evening.
Buonasera.
boo-O-na-SEH-ra.

What's happening?
Che succede?
Ke soo-CHEH-deh?

Happy holidays!
Buone vacanze!
boo-O-neh va-KAN-zeh!

Are you alright?
Stai bene?
STA-ee BEH-neh?

Merry Christmas!
Buon natale!
boo-ON na-TA-leh!

Where have you been hiding?
Ma dove sei finito?
ma DO-veh SEH-ee fee-NEE-to?

Happy New Year!
Buon anno nuovo!
boo-ON AN-no noo-O-vo!

How is your night?
Come va la serata?
KO-meh VA la seh-RA-ta?

What have you been up to all these years?
Che cosa hai fatto in tutti questi anni?
ke KO-sa A-ee FAT-to in TOOT-tee KWES-tee AN-nee?

When was the last time we saw each other?
Quand'è stata l'ultima volta che ci siamo visti?
kwand-EH STA-ta LOOL-tee-ma VOL-ta ke chee see-A-mo VEES-tee?

It's been ages since I've seen you.
Non ci vediamo da una vita.
non chi veh-dee-A-mo da OO-na VEE-ta.

How have things been going since I saw you last?
Cosa hai fatto da quando ci siamo visti l'ultima volta?
KO-sa A-ee FAT-to da KWAN-do chee see-A-mo VEES-tee LOOL-tee-ma VOL-ta?

What have you been up to?
Cos'hai combinato nel frattempo?
kos-A-ee kom-bee-NA-to nel frat-TEM-po?

How are you doing?
Come te la passi?
KO-me the la PAS-see?

Goodbye.
Addio.
ad-DEE-o.

Are you okay?
Stai bene?
STA-ee BEH-neh?

How's life been treating you?
Come ti va la vita?
KO-me tee VA la VEE-ta?

I'm sorry.
Mi dispiace.
mee dis-pee-A-cheh.

Excuse me.
Scusami.
SKOO-sa-mee.

See you later!
Ci vediamo più tardi!
chee veh-dee-AH-mo PEW TAR-dee!

What's your name?
Come ti chiami?
KO-meh tee kee-A-mee?

My name is Bill.
Mi chiamo Bill.
mee kee-A-mo Bill.

Pleased to meet you.
Piacere di conoscerti.
pee-a-CHEH-reh dee ko-NO-sher-tee.

How do you do?
Come stai?
KO-meh STA-ee?

How are things?
Come vanno le cose?
KO-meh VAN-no leh KO-seh?

You're welcome.
Prego.
PREH-go.

It's good to see you.
Che bello vederti.
ke BEL-lo ve-DER-tee.

How have you been?
Come te la stai cavando?
KO-meh teh la STA-ee ka-VAN-do?

Nice to meet you.
Piacere di conoscerti.
pee-a-CHEH-reh dee ko-NO-sher-tee.

Fine, thanks. And you?
Bene, grazie. E tu?
BEH-neh, GRA-zee-eh. eh TOO?

Good day to you.
Una buona giornata a te.
OO-na boo-O-na gee-or-NA-ta a teh.

Come in, the door is open.
Entra pure, la porta è aperta.
EN-tra POO-reh, la POR-ta eh a-PER-ta.

My wife's name is Sheila.
Il nome di mia moglie* è Sheila.
eel NO-meh dee MEE-a MOL-lee-eh eh Sheila.

　　*NOTE: Raise your tongue towards the palate while pronouncing "L".

I've been looking for you!
Stavo proprio cercando te!
STA-vo PRO-pree-o cher-KAN-do TEH!

Allow me to introduce myself. My name is Earl.
Permettetemi di presentarmi. Mi chiamo Earl.
per-met-TEH-teh-mee dee pre-sen-TAR-mee. mee kee-A-mo Earl.

I hope you have enjoyed your weekend!
Spero ti sia goduto il fine settimana!
SPE-ro tee SEE-a go-DOO-to eel FEE-neh set-tee-MA-na!

It's great to hear from you.
Che bello avere tue notizie.
ke BEL-lo a-VEH-reh TOO-eh no-TEE-zee-eh.

I hope you are having a great day.
Spero che tu stia trascorrendo una bella giornata.
SPEH-ro ke TOO STEE-a tras-kor-REN-do oo-na BEL-la gee-or-NA-ta.

Thank you for your help.
Grazie dell'aiuto.
GRA-zee-eh del-la-ee-OO-to.

DATE AND TIME

January
Gennaio
jen-NA-ee-o

February
Febbraio
feb-BRA-ee-o

March
Marzo
MAR-zo

April
Aprile
a-PREE-leh

May
Maggio
MAJ-jee-oh

June
Giugno*
jee-OO-nee-o

*NOTE: Raise your tongue towards the palate while pronouncing "N"

July
Luglio*
LOOL-lee-o

*NOTE: Raise your tongue towards the palate while pronouncing "L"

August
Agosto
a-GOS-to

September
Settembre
set-TEM-breh

October
Ottobre
ot-TO-breh

November
Novembre
no-VEM-breh

December
Dicembre
dee-CHEM-breh

What month is it?
Che mese è?
ke ME-seh eh?

At what time?
A che ora?
a keh O-ra?

Do you observe daylight savings time?
Rispetti l'ora legale?
ris-PET-tee LO-ra leh-GA-leh?

The current month is January.
Il mese in corso è gennaio.
eel ME-seh in KOR-so eh jen-NA-ee-o.

What day of the week is it?
Che giorno della settimana è?
ke gee-OR-no DEL-la set-tee-MA-na eh?

Is today Tuesday?
Oggi è martedì?
OJ-jee eh mar-teh-DEE?

Today is Monday.
Oggi è lunedì.
OJ-jee eh loo-neh-DEE.

Is this the month of January?
Questo è il mese di gennaio?
KWES-to eh eel ME-seh dee jen-NA-ee-o?

It is five minutes past one.
È l'una e cinque.
eh LOO-na eh CHIN-kweh.

It is ten minutes past one.
È l'una e dieci.
eh LOO-na eh dee-EH-chee.

It is ten till one.
È l'una meno dieci.
eh LOO-na MEH-no dee-EH-chee.

It is half past one.
È l'una e mezza.
eh LOO-na eh MEZ-za.

What time is it?
Che ora è?
keh O-ra eh?

When does the sun go down?
A che ora tramonta il sole?
ah keh O-ra tra-MON-ta eel SO-leh?

It's the third of November.
È il tre novembre.
eh eel TREH no-VEM-breh.

When does it get dark?
Quando fa buio?
KWAN-do fa BOO-ee-o?

What is today's date?
Che giorno è oggi?
ke jee-OR-no eh OJ-jee?

What time does the shoe store open?
A che ora apre il negozio di scarpe?
ah keh O-ra A-preh eel neh-GO-zee-o dee SKAR-peh?

Is today a holiday?
Oggi è un giorno di vacanza?
OJ-jee eh oon jee-OR-no dee va-KAN-za?

When is the next holiday?
Quand'è la prossima vacanza?
kwand-EH la PROS-see-ma va-KAN-za?

I will meet you at noon.
Ci vediamo a mezzogiorno.
chee veh-dee-A-mo a mez-zo-jee-OR-no.

I will meet you later tonight.
Ci vediamo più tardi in serata.
chee veh-dee-A-mo PEW TAR-dee in seh-RA-ta.

My appointment is in ten minutes.
Il mio appuntamento è tra dieci minuti.
eel MEE-o ap-poon-ta-MEN-to eh tra dee-EH-chee mee-NOO-tee.

Can we meet in half an hour?
Ci possiamo vedere tra mezz'ora?
chee pos-see-A-mo veh-DEH-reh tra mez-ZO-ra?

I will see you in March.
Ci vediamo a marzo.
chee veh-dee-A-mo a MAR-zo.

The meeting is scheduled for the twelfth.
L'appuntamento è fissato per il dodici.
lap-poon-ta-MEN-to eh fees-SA-to per eel DO-dee-chee.

Can we set up the meeting for noon tomorrow?
Possiamo fissare l'appuntamento per domani a mezzogiorno?
pos-see-A-mo fees-SA-reh lap-poon-ta-MEN-to per do-MA-nee a mez-zo-jee-OR-no?

What time will the cab arrive?
A che ora arriva il taxi?
a keh O-ra ar-REE-va eel taxi?

Can you be here by midnight?
Puoi essere qui a mezzanotte?
poo-O-ee ES-seh-reh KWEE a mez-za-NOT-teh?

The grand opening is scheduled for three o'clock.
L'inaugurazione è fissata per le tre.
lee-na-oo-goo-ra-zee-O-neh EH fees-SA-ta per leh TREH.

When is your birthday?
Quand'è il tuo compleanno?
kwand-EH eel TOO-o kom-pleh-AN-no?

My birthday is on the second of June.
Il mio compleanno è il due giugno*.
eel MEE-o kom-pleh-AN-no EH eel DOO-eh jee-OO-nee-o.

This place opens at ten a.m.
Questo posto apre alle dieci del mattino.
KWES-to POS-to a-preh AL-leh dee-EH-chee del mat-TEE-no.

From what time?
A partire da che ora?
a par-TEE-reh da keh O-ra?

Sorry, it is already too late at night.
Mi spiace, è già troppo tardi.
mee spee-A-cheh, EH jee-A TROP-po TAR-dee.

COMMON QUESTIONS

Do you speak English?
Parli inglese?
PAR-lee in-GLEH-seh?

What is your hobby?
Qual è il tuo hobby?
kwal-EH eel TOO-o hobby?

What language do you speak?
Che lingua parli?
ke LEEN-goo-a PAR-lee?

Was it hard?
È stata dura?
eh STA-ta DOO-ra?

Can you help me?
Mi puoi aiutare?
mee poo-O-ee a-ee-oo-TA-reh?

Where can I find help?
Dove posso trovare aiuto?
DO-veh POS-so tro-VA-reh a-ee-OO-to?

Where are we right now?
Dove siamo in questo momento?
DO-veh see-A-mo in KWES-to mo-MEN-to?

Where were you last night?
Dov'eri ieri sera?
do-VEH-ree ee-EH-ree SEH-ra?

What type of a tree is that?
Che tipo di albero è quello?
ke TEE-po dee AL-be-ro EH- KWEL-lo?

Do you plan on coming back here again?
Pensi di ritornare qui?
PEN-see dee ree-tor-NA-re KWEE?

What kind of an animal is that?
Che tipo di animale è quello?
ke TEE-po dee a-nee-MA-leh EH KWEL-lo?

Is that animal dangerous?
Quell'animale è pericoloso?
KWEL a-nee-MA-leh EH peh-ree-ko-LO-so?

Is it available?
È disponibile?
EH dis-po-NEE-bee-leh?

Can we come see it?
Possiamo venire a vederlo?
pos-see-A-mo veh-NEE-reh a veh-DER-lo?

Where do you live?
Dove vivi?
DO-veh VEE-vee?

Earl, what city are you from?
Earl, da che città provieni?
Earl, da keh chit-TA pro-vee-EH-nee?

Is it a very large city?
È una città molto grande?
eh OO-nah chit-TA MOL-to GRAN-deh?

Is there another available bathroom?
C'è un altro bagno* disponibile?
CHEH oon AL-tro BA-nee-oh dis-po-NEE-bee-leh?

How was your trip?
Com'è andato il viaggio?
kom-EH an-DA-to eel vee-AJ-jee-oh?

31

Is the bathroom free?
È libero il bagno* ?
EH LEE-beh-ro eel BA-nee-oh?

How are you feeling?
Come ti senti?
KO-meh tee SEN-tee?

Do you have any recommendations?
Hai dei consigli*?
A-ee DEH-ee kon-SEEL-lee?

When did you first come to China?
Quando sei venuto in Cina per la prima volta?
KWAN-do SEH-ee veh-NOO-to in CHEE-na per la PREE-ma VOL-ta?

Were you born here?
Sei nato qui?
SEH-ee NA-to KWEE?

Come join me for the rest of the vacation.
Unisciti a me per il resto della vacanza.
oo-NEE-shee-tee a MEH per eel RES-to DEL-la va-KAN-za.

What times do the shops open in this area?
A che ora aprono i negozi qui in zona?
a keh O-ra A-pro-no ee neh-GO-zee KWEE in ZO-na?

Is there tax-free shopping available?
Ci sono negozi tax free disponibili?
chee SO-no neh-GO-zee tax free dis-po-NEE-bee-lee?

Where can I change currency?
Dove posso cambiare la valuta?
DO-veh POS-so kam-bee-A-reh la va-LOO-ta?

Is it legal to drink in this area?
È legale bere in quest'area?
EH leh-GA-leh BEH-reh in kwes-TA-reh-ah?

Can I smoke in this area?
Posso fumare in quest'area?
POS-so foo-MA-reh in kwes-TA-reh-ah?

What about this?
Cosa ne dici?
KOS-a neh dee-CHEE?

Can I park here?
Posso parcheggiare qui?
POS-so par-kej-JA-reh KWEE?

Have you gotten used to living in Spain by now?
Ti sei abituato a vivere in Spagna* ora?
tee SEH-ee a-bee-too-AH-to a VEE-veh-reh in SPA-nee-a OH-ra?

How much does it cost to park here?
Quanto costa parcheggiare qui?
KWAN-to KOS-ta par-kej-JA-reh KWEE?

How long can I park here?
Per quanto tempo posso parcheggiare qui?
per KWAN-to TEM-po POS-so par-kej-JA-reh KWEE?

Where can I get some directions?
Dove posso ottenere alcune indicazioni?
DO-veh POS-so ot-teh-NEH-reh al-KOO-neh in-dee-ka-zee-O-nee?

Can you point me in the direction of the bridge?
Può indicarmi la direzione per raggiungere il ponte?
poo-O in-dee-KAR-mee la dee-re-zee-O-ne per raj-JOON-jeh-reh eel PON-teh?

What can I do here for fun?
Cosa posso fare per divertirmi qui?
KO-meh POS-so FA-re per dee-ver-TEER-mee KWEE?

Is this a family friendly place?
È un posto per famiglie*?
EH oon POS-to per fa-MEEL-lee-eh?

Are kids allowed here?
I bambini sono autorizzati a stare qui?
ee bam-BEE-nee SO-no a-oo-to-riz-ZA-tee a STA-reh KWEE?

Where can I find the park?
Dove posso trovare il parco?
DO-veh POS-so tro-VA-re eel PAR-ko?

How do I get back to my hotel?
Come torno al mio hotel?
KO-meh TOR-no al MEE-oh hotel?

Where can I get some medicine?
Dove posso acquistare delle medicine?
DO-ve POS-so a-kwee-STA-reh DEL-leh meh-dee-CHEE-neh?

Is my passport safe here?
Il mio passaporto è al sicuro qui?
eel MEE-o pas-sa-POR-to EH al see-KOO-ro KWEE?

Do you have a safe for my passport and belongings?
C'è una cassaforte per il mio passaporto e per i miei effetti personali?
CHEH OO-na kas-sa-FOR-teh per eel MEE-o pas-sa-POR-to eh per ee mee-EH-ee ef-FET-tee per-so-NA-lee?

Is it safe to be here past midnight?
Questo posto è sicuro dopo la mezzanotte?
KWES-to POS-to EH see-KOO-ro DO-po la mez-za-NOT-teh?

When is the best time to visit this shop?
Quand'è meglio* visitare questo negozio?
kwan-DEH MEL-lee-o vee-see-TA-reh KWES-to neh-GO-zee-o?

What is the best hotel in the area?
Qual è il miglior* hotel in zona?
kwal-EH eel meel-lee-OR hotel in KWES-ta ZO-na?

What attractions are close to my hotel?
Quali attrazioni ci sono vicino al mio hotel?
KWA-lee at-tra-zee-O-nee chee SO-no vee-CHEE-no al MEE-o hotel?

Do you have any advice for tourists?
Ha qualche consiglio* per i turisti?
a KWAL-keh kon-SEEL-lee-o per ee too-REES-tee?

Do you have a list of the top things to do in the area?
Ha una lista delle migliori* cose da fare in questa zona?
a OO-na LEES-ta DEL-leh meel-lee-O-ree KO-seh da FA-reh in KWES-ta ZO-na?

What do I need to pack to go there?
Cosa devo portarmi dietro per andare lì?
KO-sa DEH-vo por-TAR-mee dee-EH-tro per an-DA-reh LEE?

Can you recommend me some good food to eat?
Mi può consigliare* qualcosa di buono da mangiare?
mee poo-O kon-SEEL-lee-a-reh kwal-KO-sa dee boo-O-no da man-jee-A-reh?

What should I do with my time here?
Come posso trascorrere il tempo qui?
KO-me POS-so tras-KOR-reh-reh eel TEM-po KWEE?

What is the cheapest way to get from my hotel to the shop?
Qual è il modo più economico per andare dal mio hotel al negozio?
kwal-EH eel MO-do PEW eh-ko-NO-mee-ko per an-DA-re dal MEE-o hotel al ne-GO-zee-o?

What do you think of my itinerary?
Cosa ne pensi del mio itinerario?
KO-sa neh PEN-see del MEE-o ee-tee-neh-RA-ree-o?

Does my phone work in this country?
Il mio telefono funziona in questo paese?
eel MEE-o teh-LEH-fo-no foon-zee-O-na in KWES-to pa-EH-seh?

What is the best route to get to my hotel?
Qual è la strada migliore* per arrivare al mio hotel?
kwal-EH la STRA-da meel-lee-O-reh per ar-ree-VA-reh al MEE-o hotel?

Will the weather be okay for outside activities?
Il tempo sarà adatto alle attività all'aperto?
eel TEM-po sa-RA a-DAT-to AL-leh at-tee-vee-TA all-a-PER-to?

Was that rude?
È stato così scortese?
EH STA-to ko-SEE SKOR-teh-seh?

Where should I stay away from?
Da cosa dovrei tenermi lontano?
da KO-sa dov-REH-ee te-NER-mee lon-TA-no?

What is the best dive site in the area?
Qual è il miglior posto per fare immersioni in zona?
kwal-EH eel mee-lee-O-reh POS-to per FA-re EEm-MEHR- see-O-nehin ZO-na?

What is the best beach in the area?
Qual è la spiaggia migliore* in questa zona?
kwal-EH la spee-AJ-jee-a meel-lee-O-reh in KWES-ta ZO-na?

Do I need reservations?
Devo prenotare?
DE-vo pre-no-TA-reh?

I need directions to the best local food.
Mi servono indicazioni per il miglior* cibo locale.
mee SER-vo-no een-dee-ka-zee-O-nee per eel meel-lee-OR CHEE-bo lo-KA-leh.

What's your name?
Come ti chiami?
KO-meh tee kee-A-mee?

Where is the nearest place to eat?
Dove si trova il posto più vicino per mangiare?
DO-veh see tro-VA eel POS-to PEW vee-CHEE-no per man-jee-A-reh?

Where is the nearest hotel?
Dov'è l'hotel più vicino?
do-VEH lo-TEL PEW vee-CHEE-no?

Where is transportation?
Dove trovo i mezzi di trasporto?
DO-veh TRO-vo ee MEZ-zee dee tras-POR-to?

How much is this?
Quant'è?
kwan-TEH?

Do you pay tax here?
Si pagano le tasse qui?
see PA-ga-no le TAS-seh KWEE?

What types of payment are accepted?
Quali tipi di pagamento sono accettati?
KWA-lee TEE-pee dee pa-ga-MEN-to SO-no a-chet-TA-tee?

Can you help me read this?
Mi può aiutare a leggere questo?
mee poo-O a-ee-oo-TA-reh a LEJ-jeh-reh KWES-to?

What languages do you speak?
Che lingue parli?
keh LEEN-goo-eh PAR-lee?

Is it difficult to speak English?
È difficile parlare inglese?
EH dif-FEE-chee-leh par-LA-reh in-GLEH-seh?

What does that mean?
Cosa significa*?
KO-sa seen-NEE-fee-ka?

What is your name?
Come ti chiami?
KO-meh tee kee-A-mee?

Do you have a lighter?
Hai un accendino?
A-ee oon a-chen-DEE-no?

Do you have a match?
Hai un fiammifero?
A-ee oon fee-am-MEE-fe-ro?

Is this a souvenir from your country?
Questo è un souvenir del tuo paese?
KWES-to EH oon souvenir del TOO-oh pa-EH-seh?

What is this?
Cos'è questo?
kos-EH KWES-to?

Can I ask you a question?
Posso fare una domanda?
POS-so FA-re OO-na do-MAN-da?

Where is the safest place to store my travel information?
Qual è il posto più sicuro dove mettere le mie informazioni di viaggio?
kwal-EH eel POS-to PEW see-KOO-ro DO-veh MET-te-reh leh MEE-eh in-for-ma-zee-OH-nee dee vee-AJ-jee-o?

Will you come along with me?
Verrai con me?
ver-RA-ee kon MEH?

Is this your first time here?
È la tua prima volta qui?
EH la TOO-a PREE-ma VOL-ta KWEE?

What is your opinion on the matter?
Qual è la tua opinione in merito?
kwal-EH la TOO-a o-pee-nee-O-neh in MEH-ree-to?

Will this spoil if I leave it out too long?
Si rovina se lo lascio fuori troppo a lungo?
see ro-VEE-na seh lo LA-shee-o foo-O-ree TROP-po a LOON-go?

What side of the sidewalk do I walk on?
Su che lato del marciapiede si può camminare?
soo keh LA-to del mar-chee-a-pee-EH-deh see poo-O kam-mee-NA-reh?

What do those lights mean?
Cosa significano* quelle luci?
KO-sa seen-NEE-fee-ka-no KWEL-leh LOO-chee?

Can I walk up these stairs?
Posso salire su queste scale?
POS-so sa-LEE-reh soo KWES-teh SKA-leh?

Is that illegal here?
Qui, questo è illegale?
KWEE, KWES-to EH eel-leh-GA-leh?

How much trouble would I get in if I did that?
Che tipo di problema avrei se lo facessi?
keh TEE-po dee pro-BLEH-ma a-VREH-ee seh lo fa-CHES-see?

Why don't we all go together?
Perché non andiamo tutti assieme?
per-KEH non an-dee-A-mo TOOT-tee as-see-EH-meh?

May I throw away waste here?
Posso gettare l'immondizia qui?
POS-so jet-TA-reh leem-mon-DEE-zee-a KWEE?

Where is the recycle bin?
Dov'è il bidone dell'immondizia?
do-VEH eel bee-DO-neh del-leem-mon-DEE-zee-a?

WHEN SOMEONE IS BEING RUDE

Please, close your mouth while chewing that.
Per favore, chiudi la bocca mentre mastichi.
per fa-VO-reh, kee-OO-dee la BOK-ka MEN-treh MAS-tee-kee.

Don't ask me again, please.
Non me lo chiedere di nuovo, ti prego.
non meh lo kee-EH-deh-reh dee noo-O-vo, tee PREH-go.

I'm not paying for that.
Non pagherò per quello.
non pa-geh-RO per KWEL-lo.

Leave me alone or I am calling the authorities.
Lasciami in pace o chiamo la polizia.
LA-shee-a-mee in PA-cheh o kee-A-mo la po-lee-ZEE-a.

Hurry up!
Sbrigati!
SBREE-ga-tee!

Stop bothering me!
Smettila di infastidirmi!
SMET-tee-la dee in-fas-TEE-dEER-mee!

Don't bother me, please!
Non mi importunare, per favore!
non meen-por-too-NA-reh, per fa-VO-reh!

Are you content?
Sei soddisfatto?
SEH-ee sod-dees-FAT-to?

I'm walking away, please don't follow me.
Me ne vado, ti prego di non seguirmi.
meh neh VA-do, tee PRE-go dee non se-goo-EER-mee.

40

You stole my shoes and I would like them back.
Mi hai rubato le scarpe e le vorrei indietro.
mee A-ee roo-BA-to leh SKAR-peh eh leh vor-REH-ee in-dee-EH-tro.

You have the wrong person.
Hai sbagliato* persona.
a-EE sbal-lee-AH-to PER-so-NA.

I think you are incorrect.
Credo ti stia sbagliando*.
KREH-do see STEE-a sbal-lee-AN-do.

Stop waking me up!
Lasciami dormire!
LA-shee-a-mee dor-MEE-re!

You're talking too much.
Stai parlando troppo!
STA-ee par-LAN-do TROP-po!

That hurts!
Questo fa male!
KWES-to fa MA-leh!

I need you to apologize.
Devi scusarti.
DEH-vee skoo-SAR-tee.

Stay away from my children!
Stai lontano dai miei bambini!
STA-ee lon-TA-no DA-ee mee-EH-ee bam-BEE-nee!

Don't touch me.
Non mi toccare.
non mee tok-KA-reh.

I would appreciate it if you didn't take my seat.
Apprezzerei se non mi prendessi il posto.
ap-prez-zeh-REH-ee seh non mee pren-DES-see eel POS-to.

You didn't tell me that.
Non me l'hai detto.
non meh-LA-ee DET-to.

You are price gouging me.
Stai gonfiando il prezzo.
STA-ee gon-fee-AN-do eel PREZ-zo.

Please be quiet, I am trying to listen.
Fai silenzio, per favore, sto cercando di ascoltare.
FA-ee see-LEN-zee-oh, per fa-VO-reh, sto cher-KAN-do dee as-kol-TA-reh.

Don't interrupt me while I am talking.
Non mi interrompere mentre parlo.
non mee in-ter-ROM-peh-reh MEN-treh PAR-lo.

Don't sit on my car and stay away from it.
Non ti sedere nella mia macchina e stannelontano.
non tee seh-DEH-reh NEL-la MEE-a MAK-kee-na eh STAN-neh lon-TA-no.

Get out of my car.
Scendi dalla mia macchina.
SCHEN-dee DAL-la MEE-a MAK-kee-na.

Get away from me and leave me alone!
Vattene via e lasciami sola!
VAT-teh-neh VEE-ah eh LAS-chee-ah-mee SO-la!

You're being rude.
Sei maleducato.
SEH-ee ma-leh-doo-KA-to.

Please don't curse around my children.
Non dire parolacce davanti ai miei bambini.
non DEE-reh pa-ro-LA-cheh da-VAN-tee A-ee mee-EH-ee bam-BEE-nee.

Let go of me!
Lasciami andare!
LA-shee-a-mee an-DA-reh!

I'm not going to tell you again.
Non te lo dirò di nuovo.
non teh lo dee-RO dee noo-O-vo.

Don't yell at me.
Non urlarmi contro.
non oor-LAR-mee KON-tro.

Please lower your voice.
Per favore, abbassa il tono della voce.
per fa-VO-reh, ab-BAS-sa eel TO-no DEL-la VO-cheh.

What is the problem?
Qual è il problema?
kwal-EH eel pro-BLEH-ma?

I would appreciate if you didn't take pictures of me.
Vorrei che non mi facessi delle foto.
vor-REH-ee keh non mee fa-CHES-see DEL-le FO-to.

I am very disappointed in the way you are behaving.
Sono molto deluso dal modo in cui ti stai comportando.
SO-no MOL-to deh-LOO-so dal MO-do in KOO-ee tee STA-ee kom-por-TAN-do.

Watch where you are walking!
Guarda dove cammini!
GWAR-da DO-ve kam-MEE-nee!

He just bumped into me!
Lui mi ha urtato!
LO-ee mee A oor-TA-to!

MEDICAL

I would like to set up an appointment with my doctor.
Vorrei prenotare un appuntamento col mio dottore.
vor-REH-ee preh-no-TA-reh oon ap-poon-ta-MEN-to kol MEE-o dot-TO-reh.

I am a new patient and need to fill out forms.
Sono un paziente nuovo e devo compilare il questionario.
SO-no oon pa-zee-EN-teh noo-O-vo eh DEH-vo kom-pee-LA-reh eel kwes-tee-o-NA-ree-o.

I am allergic to certain medications.
Sono allergico a certi medicinali.
SO-no al-LER-jee-ko a CHER-tee meh-dee-chee-NA-lee.

That is where it hurts.
È qui che fa male.
EH KWEE ke fa MA-leh.

I have had the flu for three weeks.
Ho avuto l'influenza per tre settimane.
O a-VOO-to lin-floo-EN-za per TREH set-tee-MA-neh.

It hurts when I walk on that foot.
Mi fa male quando cammino su quel piede.
mee fa MA-leh KWAN-do kam-MEE-no soo KWEL pee-EH-deh.

When is my next appointment?
Quand'è il mio prossimo appuntamento?
kwan-DEH eel MEE-o PROS-see-mo ap-poon-ta-MEN-to?

Does my insurance cover this?
La mia assicurazione lo copre?
la MEE-a as-see-koo-ra-zee-O-neh lo KO-preh?

Do you want to take a look at my throat?
Può dare un'occhiata alla mia gola?
poo-O DA-reh oon ok-kee-A-ta AL-la MEE-a GO-la?

Do I need to fast before going there?
Devo andarci a digiuno?
DE-vo an-DAR-chee a dee-joo-no?

Is there a generic version of this medicine?
C'è una versione generica di questo medicinale?
CHEH OO-na ver-see-O-neh jeh-NEH-ree-ka dee KWES-to meh-dee-chee-NA-leh?

I need to get back on dialysis.
Devo tornare a fare la dialisi.
de-vo tor-NA-re a FA-re LA dee-A-lee-see.

My blood type is A.
Il mio gruppo sanguigno* è A.
eel MEE-o GROOP-po san-GWEEN-nee-o EH A.

I will be more than happy to donate blood.
Sarei ben lieto di donare il sangue.
sa-REH-ee ben lee-EH-to dee do-NA-re eel SAN-gweh.

I have been feeling dizzy.
Mi sento stordito.
mee SEN-to stor-DEE-to.

The condition is getting worse.
La malattia sta peggiorando.
la ma-lat-TEE-ah sta pej-jo-RAN-do.

The medicine has made the condition a little better, but it is still there.
Il medicinale ha migliorato* un po' la malattia, ma è ancora presente.
eel meh-dee-chee-NA-leh a meel-lee-o-RA-to oon PO la ma-lat-TEE-a, ma EH an-KO-ra preh-SEN-teh.

Is my initial health examination tomorrow?
Il mio esame medico è per domani?
eel MEE-o eh-SA-meh MEH-dee-ko EH per do-MA-nee?

I would like to switch doctors.
Vorrei cambiare dottore.
vor-REH-ee kam-bee-A-reh dot-TO-reh.

Can you check my blood pressure?
Può controllare la mia pressione sanguigna*?
poo-O kon-trol-LA-re la MEE-a pres-see-O-neh san-GWEEN-nee-a?

I have a fever that won't go away.
La febbre non vuole andare via.
la FEB-breh non voo-O-leh an-DA-reh VEE-a.

I think my arm is broken.
Credo che il mio braccio sia rotto.
KREH-do ke eel MEE-o BRA-chee-o SEE-a ROT-to.

I think I have a concussion.
Credo di avere una commozione cerebrale.
KREH-do dee a-VEH-re OO-na kom-moz-zee-O-neh cheh-reh-BRA-leh.

My eyes refuse to focus.
I miei occhi non riescono a mettere a fuoco.
ee mee-EH-ee OK-kee non ree-ES-ko-no a MET-eh-reh ah foo-O-ko.

I have double vision.
Ci vedo doppio.
chi VEH-do DOP-pee-o.

Is surgery the only way to fix this?
Un intervento chirurgico è l'unico modo per guarire?
oon een-ter-VEN-to kee-ROOR-jee-ko EH LOO-nee-ko MO-do per gwa-REE-reh?

Who are you referring me to?
Da chi mi stai mandando?
da kee mee STA-ee man-DAN-do?

Where is the waiting room?
Dov'è la sala d'attesa?
do-VEH la SA-la dat-TEH-sa?

Can I bring someone with me into the office?
Posso portare qualcuno con me nello studio del medico?
POS-so por-TA-reh kwal-KOO-no kon MEH NEL-lo STOO-dee-o del MEH-dee-ko?

I need help filling out these forms.
Ho bisogno* d'aiuto per compilare il questionario.
o bee-SON-nee-o dee a-ee-OO-to per kom-pee-LA-reh eel kwes-tee-o-NA-ree-o.

Do you take Cobra as an insurance provider?
Hai scelto Cobra come compagnia* di assicurazioni?
A-ee SHEL-to KO-bra KO-me com-pan-NEE-a dee as-see-koo-ra-zee-O-nee?

What is my co payment?
Qual è la mia assicurazione medica?
kwal-EH la MEE-a as-see-koo-ra-zee-O-neh MEH-dee-ka?

What forms of payment do you accept?
Che tipo di pagamenti accettate?
keh TEE-po dee pa-ga-MEN-tee a-chet-TA-teh?

Do you have a payment plan or is it all due now?
Posso pagare a rate o devo pagare tutto ora?
POS-so pa-GA-reh a RA-teh O DEH-vo pa-GA-re TOOT-to O-ra?

My old doctor prescribed something different.
Il mio vecchio dottore mi ha prescritto qualcosa di diverso.
eel MEE-o VEK-kee-o dot-TO-reh mee A pres-KREET-to kwal-KO-sa dee dee-VER-so.

Will you take a look at my leg?
Può dare un'occhiata alla mia gamba?
poo-O DA-re oon ok-kee-A-ta AL-la MEE-a GAM-ba?

I need to be referred to a gynecologist.
Ho bisogno* di essere visitata da un ginecologo.
o bee-SON-nee-o dee ES-seh-reh vee-see-TA-ta da oon jee-neh-KO-lo-go.

I am unhappy with the medicine you prescribed me.
Non mi trovo bene con la medicina che mi ha prescritto.
non mee TRO-vo BEH-ne kon la meh-dee-CHEE-na keh mee a pres-KREET-to.

Do you see patients on the weekend?
Visita i pazienti durante il fine settimana?
VEE-see-ta ee pa-zee-EN-tee eel FEE-neh set-tee-MA-na?

I need a good therapist.
Ho bisogno* di un buon fisioterapeuta.
o bee-SON-nee-o dee oon boo-ON FEE-see-o-teh-RAP-EH-oo-TA.

How long will it take me to rehab this injury?
Quanto tempo ci vorrà prima di riprendermi da questo infortunio?
KWAN-to TEM-po chee vor-RA PREE-ma dee ree-PREN-der-mee da KWES-to in-for-TOO-nee-o?

I have not gone to the bathroom in over a week.
Non vado in bagno* da più di una settimana.
non VA-do in BAN-nee-o da PEW dee OO-na set-tee-MA-na.

I am constipated and feel bloated.
Mi sento costipato e gonfio.
mee SEN-to ko-stee-PA-to eh GON-fee-o.

It hurts when I go to the bathroom.
Mi fa male quando vado in bagno*.
mee fa MA-leh KWAN-do VA-do in BAN-nee-o.

I have not slept well at all since getting here.
Non dormo bene da quando sono arrivato qui.
non DOR-mo BE-ne da KWAN-do SO-no ar-ree-VA-to KWEE.

Do you have any pain killers?
Ha qualche antidolorifico?
a KWAL-keh an-tee-do-lo-REE-fee-ko?

I am allergic to that medicine.
Sono allergico a quella medicina.
SO-no al-LER-jee-ko a KWEL-la me-dee-CHEE-na.

How long will I be under observation?
Per quanto tempo dovrò stare sotto osservazione?
per KWAN-to TEM-po do-VRO STA-re SOT-to os-ser-va-zee-O-neh?

I have a toothache.
Ho mal di denti.
o MAL dee DEN-tee.

Do I need to see a dentist?
Devo andare dal dentista?
DE-vo an-DA-reh dal den-TEE-sta?

Does my insurance cover dental?
La mia assicurazione copre un intervento ai denti?
la MEE-a as-see-koo-ra-zee-O-neh KO-preh oon in-ter-VEN-to A-ee DEN-tee?

My diarrhea won't go away.
La mia diarrea non se ne vuole andare.
la MEE-a dee-ar-REH-a non seh neh voo-O-leh an-DA-reh.

Can I have a copy of the receipt for my insurance?
Posso avere una copia della ricevuta per la mia assicurazione?
POS-so a-VEH-reh OO-na KO-pee-a DEL-la ree-cheh-VOO-ta per la MEE-a as-see-koo-ra-zee-O-neh?

I need a pregnancy test.
Ho bisogno* di un test di gravidanza.
o bee-SON-nee-o dee oon test dee gra-vee-DAN-za.

I think I may be pregnant.
Penso che potrei essere incinta.
PEN-so keh pot-REH-ee ES-seh-reh een-CHEEN-ta.

Can we please see a pediatrician?
Possiamo, per favore, vedere un pediatra?
pos-see-A-mo per fa-VO-reh veh-DEH-reh oon peh-dee-A-tra?

I have had troubles breathing.
Ho delle difficoltà a respirare.
o DEL-leh deef-fee-kol-TA a res-pee-RA-reh.

My sinuses are acting up.
Ho la sinusite.
o la see-noo-SEE-teh.

Will I still be able to breastfeed?
Sarò ancora in grado di allattare al seno?
sa-RO an-KO-ra in GRA-do dee al-lat-TA-reh al SEH-no?

How long do I have to stay in bed?
Per quanto tempo dovrò stare a letto?
per KWAN-to TEM-po do-VRO STA-reh a LET-to?

How long do I have to stay under hospital care?
Per quanto tempo dovrò stare in ospedale?
per KWAN-to TEM-po do-VRO STA-reh in os-peh-DA-leh?

Is it contagious?
È contagioso?
eh kon-ta-jee-O-so?

How far along am I?
Quanto tempo ci vorrà?
KWAN-to TEM-po chee vor-RA?

What did the x ray say?
Cosa dicono i raggi x?
KO-sa DEE-ko-no ee RAJ-jee EEKS?

Can I walk without a cane?
Posso camminare senza bastone?
POS-so kam-mee-NA-reh SEN-za bas-TO-ne?

Is the wheelchair necessary?
La sedia a rotelle è necessaria?
la SE-dee-a a ro-TEL-leh EH neh-ches-SA-ree-a?

Am I in the right area of the hospital?
Sono nella zona giusta dell'ospedale?
SO-no NEL-la ZO-na jee-OOS-ta dell-os-peh-DA-leh?

Where is the front desk receptionist?
Dove posso trovare l'accettazione?
DO-ve POS-so tro-VA-reh la-chet-ta-zee-O-neh?

I would like to go to a different waiting area.
Vorrei andare in un'altra sala d'attesa.
vor-REH-ee an-DA-reh in oon-AL-tra SA-la dat-TEH-sa.

Can I have a change of sheets please?
Posso avere delle lenzuola nuove?
POS-so a-VEH-reh DEL-leh len-zoo-O-la noo-O-veh?

Excuse me nurse, what is your name?
Mi scusi infermiera, qual è il suo nome?
mee SKOO-see in-fer-mee-EH-ra, kwal-EH eel SOO-o NO-meh?

Who is the doctor in charge here?
Chi è il medico responsabile, qui?
kee EH eel MEH-dee-ko res-pon-SA-bee-leh KWEE?

I need some assistance, please.
Avrei bisogno* di assistenza, per favore.
a-VREH-ee bee-SON-nee-o dee as-sees-TEN-za, per fa-VO-reh.

Will my recovery affect my ability to do work?
La mia convalescenza avrà effetti sul mio lavoro?
la MEE-a kon-va-le-SHEN-za a-VRA ef-FET-tee sool MEE-o la-VO-ro?

How long is the estimated recovery time?
A quanto ammonta il tempo di guarigione?
a KWAN-to am-MON-ta eel TEM-po dee goo-a-ree-JO-neh?

Is that all you can do for me? There has to be another option.
È tutto quello che può fare per me? Ci dev'essere un'altra opzione.
eh TOOT-to KWEL-lo keh poo-O FA-reh per MEH? Chee dev-ES-seh-reh oon-AL-tra op-zee-O-neh.

I need help with motion sickness.
Ho bisogno* d'aiuto per il mal d'auto.
o bee-SON-nee-o dee a-ee-OO-to per eel mal-DA-oo-to.

I'm afraid of needles.
Ho paura degli* aghi.
o pa-OO-ra DEL-lee AH-ghee.

My gown is too small, I need another one.
Il mio camice è troppo piccolo, me ne serve un altro.
eel MEE-o KA-mee-cheh EH TROP-po PEEK-ko-lo, meh neh SER-veh oon-AL-tro.

Can I have extra pillows?
Posso avere un cuscino in più?
POS-so a-VEH-reh oon koo-SHEE-no in PEW?

I need assistance getting to the bathroom.
Ho bisogno* di aiuto per andare in bagno*.
o bee-SON-nee-o dee a-ee-OO-to per an-DA-reh in BAN-nee-o.

Hi, is the doctor in?
Salve, c'è il dottore?
SAL-veh, CHEH eel dot-TO-reh?

When should I schedule the next checkup?
Quando devo fissare il prossimo appuntamento?
KWAN-do DE-vo fees-SA-reh eel PROS-see-mo ap-poon-ta- MEN-to?

When can I have these stitches removed?
Quando potrò togliere* questi punti?
KWAN-do po-TRO TOL-lee-eh-reh KWES-tee POON-tee?

Do you have any special instructions while I'm in this condition?
Ha qualche istruzione speciale da darmi mentre sono in queste condizioni?
a KWAL-keh ees-troo-zee-O-neh speh-chee-A-leh da DAR-mee men-treh SO-no in KWES-teh kon-dee-zee-O-nee?

ORDERING FOOD

Can I see the menu?
Posso vedere il menu?
POS-so veh-DEH-reh eel meh-NOO?

I'm really hungry. We should eat something soon.
Sono davvero affamato. Dovremmo mangiare qualcosa a breve.
SO-no dav-VEH-ro af-fa-MA-to. do-VREM-mo man-jee-A-reh kwal-KO-sa a BREH-veh.

Can I take a look in the kitchen?
Posso dare un'occhiata in cucina?
POS-so DA-reh oon-ok-kee-A-ta in koo-CHEE-na?

Can we see the drink menu?
Possiamo vedere la lista delle bevande?
pos-see-A-mo veh-DEH-reh la LEES-ta DEL-leh beh-VAN-deh?

When can we be seated?
Quando possiamo sederci?
KWAN-do pos-see-A-mo ve-DER-chee?

This is very tender and delicious.
Questo è davvero tenero e delizioso.
KWES-to EH dav-VEH-ro TEH-neh-ro eh deh-lee-zee-O-so.

Do you serve alcohol?
Servite alcol?
ser-VEE-teh al-KO-lee-chee?

I'm afraid our party can't make it.
Temo che il nostro gruppo non ce la farà.
TEH-mo keh eel NOS-tro GROOP-po non cheh la fa-RAH.

That room is reserved for us.
Quella sala è riservata per noi.
KWEL-la SA-la EH ree-ser-VA-ta per NO-ee.

Are there any seasonal favorites that you serve?
Ci sono dei piatti di stagione particolari che servite?
chee SO-no pee-AT-tee dee sta-jee-O-neh keh ser-VEE-teh?

Do you offer discounts for kids or seniors?
Offrite sconti per bambini o anziani?
of-FREE-teh SKON-tee per bam-BEE-nee o an-zee-A-nee?

I would like it filleted.
Lo vorrei sfilettato.
lo vor-REH-ee sfee-let-TA-to.

I would like to reserve a table for a party of four.
Vorrei prenotare un tavolo per quattro persone.
vor-REH-ee pre-no-TA-re oon TA-vo-lo per KWAT-tro per-SO-neh.

I would like to place the reservation under my name.
Vorrei prenotare a mio nome.
vor-REH-ee pre-no-TA-reh a MEE-o NO-meh.

What type of alcohol do you serve?
Che tipo di alcol servite?
keh TEE-po dee AL-kol ser-VEE-teh?

Do I need a reservation?
Devo prenotare?
DE-vo pre-no-TA-reh?

What does it come with?
Con che cosa viene servito?
kon keh KO-sa vee-EH-neh ser-VEE-to?

What are the ingredients?
Quali sono gli* ingredienti?
KWA-lee SO-no lee in-greh-dee-EN-tee?

What else does the chef put in the dish?
Cos'altro mette lo chef nel piatto?
kos-AL-tro a MET-teh lo chef nel pee-AT-to?

I wonder which of these tastes better?
Chissà quale di questi avrà il miglior* sapore?
kees-SA KWA-le dee KWES-tee a-VRA eel meel-lee-OR sa-PO-reh?

That is incorrect. Our reservation was at noon.
Non è corretto. La nostra prenotazione era per mezzogiorno.
non EH kor-REH-to. la NOS-tra preh-no-ta-zee-O-neh EH-ra per mez-zo-jee-OR-no.

I would like red wine please.
Vorrei del vino rosso, per favore.
vor-REH-ee del VEE-no ROS-so, per fa-VO-reh.

Can you take the head for the soup?
Ti sei deciso per la zuppa?
tee SEH-ee deh-CHEE-so per la ZOOP-pa?

What is the most popular dish here?
Qual è il piatto più popolare qui?
kwal-EH eel pee-AT-to PEW po-po-LA-reh KWEE?

What are the specials today?
Quali sono i piatti del giorno?
KWA-lee SO-no ee pee-AT-tee del JOR-no?

What are your appetizers?
Quali sono i vostri antipasti?
KWA-lee SO-no ee VOS-tree an-tee-PAS-tee?

Please bring these out separately.
Per favore, li faccia uscire separatamente.
per fa-VO-reh, lee FA-chee-a oos-CHEE-reh seh-pa-ra-ta-MEN-teh.

Do we leave a tip?
Lasciamo una mancia?
la-shee-A-mo OO-na MAN-chee-a?

Are tips included with the bill?
La mancia è inclusa nel conto?
la MAN-chee-a EH- in-KLOO-sa nel KON-to?

Split the bill, please.
Divida il conto, per favore.
dee-VEE-da eel KON-to, per fa-VO-reh.

We are ordering separate.
Ordiniamo separatamente.
or-dee-nee-A-mo seh-pa-ra-ta-MEN-teh.

Is there an extra fee for sharing an entrée?
C'è un costo extra per condividere un antipasto?
cheh oon KOS-to extra per kon-dee-VEE-deh-reh oon an-tee-PAS-to?

Is there a local specialty that you recommend?
C'è qualche specialità locale che raccomanda?
cheh KWAL-keh spe-chee-a-lee-TA lo-KA-leh keh rak-ko-MAN-da?

This looks different from what I originally ordered.
Questo sembra diverso da quello che ho ordinato io.
KWES-to SEM-bra dee-VER-so da KWEL-lo keh o or-dee-NA-to EE-o.

Is this a self serve buffet?
Questo è un buffet self service?
KWES-to EH oon boof-FEH self-service?

I want a different waiter.
Vorrei un altro cameriere.
vor-REH-ee oon AL-tro ka-meh-ree-EH-reh.

Please move us to a different table.
Per favore, spostateci in un altro tavolo.
per fa-VO-reh, spos-TA-teh-chee in oon AL-tro TA-vo-lo.

Can we put two tables together?
Possiamo unire due tavoli?
pos-see-A-mo oo-NEE-reh DOO-eh TA-vo-lee?

My spoon is dirty. Can I have another one?
Il mio cucchiaio è sporco. Posso averne un altro?
eel MEE-o kook-kee-A-ee-o EH SPOR-ko. POS-so a-VER-neh oon-AL-tro?

We need more napkins, please.
Abbiamo bisogno* di altri tovaglioli*, per favore.
ab-bee-AH-mo bee-SON-nee-o dee AL-tree to-val-lee-O-lee, per fa-VO-reh.

I'm a vegetarian and don't eat meat.
Sono vegetariano e non mangio carne.
SO-no veh-jeh-ta-ree-A-no eh non MAN-jee-o KAR-neh.

The table next to us is being too loud. Can you say something?
Il tavolo a fianco al nostro è troppo rumoroso. Può dirgli qualcosa?
eel TA-vo-lo a fee-AN-ko al NOS-tro EH TROP-po roo-mo-RO-so. poo-O DEER-lee kwal-KO-sa?

Someone is smoking in our nonsmoking area.
Qualcuno sta fumando nella zona non fumatori.
kwal-KOO-no sta foo-MAN-do nella ZO-na non foo-ma-TO-ree.

Please seat us in a booth.
Per favore, ci faccia accomodare in un privé.
per fa-VO-reh, chee FA-chee-a ak-ko-mo-DA-reh in oon pree-VEH.

Do you have any non-alcoholic beverages?
Avete delle bevande non alcoliche?
a-VEH-teh DEL-leh beh-VAN-deh non al-KO-lee-keh?

Where is your bathroom?
Dov'è il bagno*?
dov-EH eel BAN-nee-oh?

Are you ready to order?
Siete pronti per ordinare?
see-EH-teh PRON-tee per or-dee-NA-reh?

Five more minutes, please.
Ancora cinque minuti, per favore.
an-KO-ra CHIN-kweh mee-NOO-tee, per fa-VO-reh.

What time do you close?
A che ora chiudete?
ah keh O-ra kee-oo-DEH-teh?

Is there pork in this dish? I don't eat pork.
C'è del maiale in questo piatto? Io non mangio maiale.
cheh del ma-ee-A-leh in KWES-to pee-AT-to? EE-o non MAN-jee-o ma-ee-A-leh.

Do you have any dishes for vegans?
Avete dei piatti per vegani?
a-VEH-teh DEH-ee pee-AT-tee per veh-GA-nee?

Are these vegetables fresh?
Queste verdure sono fresche?
KWES-teh ver-DOO-reh SO-no FRES-keh?

Have any of these vegetables been cooked in butter?
Alcune di queste verdure sono state cucinate nel burro?
al-KOO-neh dee KWES-teh ver-DOO-reh SO-no STA-teh koo-chee-NA-teh nel BOOR-ro?

Is this spicy?
Questo è piccante?
KWES-to EH peek-KAN-teh?

Is this sweet?
Questo è dolce?
KWES-to EH DOL-cheh?

I want more please.
Ne vorrei ancora, per favore.
neh vor-REH-ee an-KO-ra, per fa-VO-reh.

I would like a dish containing these items.
Vorrei un piatto che contenga queste cose.
vor-REH-ee oon pee-AT-to ke kon-TEN-ga KWES-teh KO-seh.

Can you make this dish light? Thank you.
Può prepararmi un piatto più leggero? Grazie.
poo-O preh-PA-ra-reh oon pee-AT-to PEW lej-JEH-ro? GRA-zee-eh.

Nothing else.
Nient'altro.
nee-en-TAL-tro.

Please clear the plates.
Per favore, portate via i piatti.
per fa-VO-reh, por-TA-teh VEE-a ee pee-AT-tee.

May I have a cup of soup?
Potrei avere una zuppa?
po-TREH-ee a-VEH-reh OO-na ZOOP-pa?

Do you have any bar snacks?
Avete degli* snack?
a-VEH-teh DEL-lee snack?

Another round, please.
Un altro giro, per favore.
oon AL-tro JEE-ro, per fa-VO-reh.

When is closing time for the bar?
A che ora chiude il bar?
a keh O-ra kee-OO-deh eel bar?

That was delicious!
Era squisito!
EH-ra SKWEE-zee-to !

Does this have alcohol in it?
Contiene alcol?
kon-tee-EH-neh AL-kol?

Does this have nuts in it?
Contiene delle nocciole?
kon-tee-EH-neh DEL-leh no-chee-O-leh?

Is this gluten free?
È senza glutine?
EH SEN-za GLOO-tee-neh?

Can I get this to go?
Posso portarlo via?
POS-so por-TAR- lo VEE-a?

May I have a refill?
Me lo potrebbe riempire di nuovo?
meh lo po-TREB-beh ree-em-PEE-reh dee noo-O-vo?

Is this dish kosher?
Questo è un piatto casalingo?
KWES-to EH oon pee-AT-to KA-sa-leen-go?

I would like to change my drink.
Vorrei cambiare il mio drink.
vor-REH-ee kam-bee-A-reh eel MEE-o drink.

My coffee is cold. Could you please warm it up?
Il mio caffé è freddo. Potrebbe scaldarmelo?
eel MEE-o kaf-FEH EH fred-do. po-TREB-beh skal-DAR-meh-lo?

Do you serve coffee?
Servite anche caffé?
ser-VEE-teh AN-keh kaf-FEH?

Can I please have cream in my coffee?
Potrei avere della panna nel mio caffé?
po-TREH-ee a-VEH-reh DEL-la PAN-na nel MEE-o kaf-FEH?

Please add extra sugar to my coffee.
Mi metta dell'altro zucchero nel caffè, per favore.
mee MET-ta dell-AL-tro ZOOK-keh-ro nel kaf-FEH, per fa-VO-reh.

I would like to have my coffee served black, no cream and no sugar.
Vorrei che il mio caffé fosse servito nero, senza panna e senza zucchero.
vor-REH-ee keh eel MEE-o kaf-FEH FOS-seh ser-VEE-to NEH-ro, SEN-za PAN-na eh SEN-za ZOOK-keh-ro.

I would like to have decaffeinated coffee, please.
Vorrei un caffé decaffeinato, per favore.
vor-REH-ee oon deh-kaf-feh-ee-NA-to, per fa-VO-reh.

Do you serve coffee flavored ice cream?
Servite del gelato al gusto di caffé?
ser-VEE-teh del jeh-LA-to al GOOS-to dee kaf-FEH?

Please put my cream and sugar on the side so that I can add it myself.
Per favore, mi metta la panna e lo zucchero a parte, così che possa
aggiungerli da solo.
per fa-VO-reh, mee MET-ta la PAN-na eh lo ZOOK-keh-ro a PAR-teh, ko-SEE keh POS-sa aj-JOON-jer-lee da SO-lo.

I would like to order an iced coffee.
Vorrei ordinare un caffé con ghiaccio.
vor-REH-ee or-dee-NA-reh oon kaf-FEH kon ghee-A-chee-o.

I would like an Espresso please.
Vorrei un espresso, per favore.
vor-REH-ee oon es-PRES-so, per fa-VO-reh.

Do you have 2% milk?
Avete latte scremato?
a-VEH-teh LAT-teh skreh-MA-to?

Do you serve soy milk?
Servite latte di soia?
ser-VEE-teh LAT-te dee SO-ee-a?

Do you have almond milk?
Avete latte di mandorla?
a-VEH-teh LAT-te di MAN-dor-la?

Are there any alternatives to the milk you serve?
Ci sono delle alternative al latte che servite?
chee SO-no DEL-leh al-ter-na-TEE-veh al LAT-teh keh ser-VEE-teh?

Please put the lemons for my tea on the side.
Per favore, vorrei il limone per il té a parte.
per fa-VO-reh, vor-REH-ee eel LAT-te per eel TEH a PAR-teh.

No lemons with my tea, thank you.
Niente limone col té, per favore.
nee-EN-teh lee-MO-neh kol TEH, per fa-VO-reh.

Is your water from the tap?
La vostra acqua è di rubinetto?
la VOS-tra AK-kwa EH dee roo-bee-NET-to?

Sparkling water, please.
Un'acqua gasata, per favore.
oon AK-kwa ga-SA-ta, per fa-VO-reh.

Can I get a diet coke?
Posso avere una *Coca* Cola Zero?
POS-so a-VEH-reh OO-na Ko-ka Ko-la ZEH-ro?

We're ready to order.
Siamo pronti per ordinare.
see-A-mo PRON-tee per or-dee-NA-reh.

Can we be seated over there instead?
Possiamo sederci anche lì?
pos-see-A-mo seh-DER-chee AN-keh LEE?

Can we have a seat outside?
Possiamo sederci fuori?
pos-see-A-mo seh-DER-chee foo-O-ree?

Please hold the salt.
Per favore, niente sale.
per fa-VO-reh, nee-EN-teh SA-leh.

This is what I would like for my main course.
Questo è quello che vorrei come portata principale.
KWES-to EH KWEL-lo keh vor-REH-ee KO-meh por-TA-ta prin-chee-PA-leh.

I would like the soup instead of the salad.
Vorrei la zuppa al posto dell'insalata.
vor-REH-ee la ZOOP-pa al POS-to dell-in-sa-LA-ta.

I'll have the chicken risotto.
Prenderò il risotto col pollo.
pren-deh-RO eel ree-SOT-to kol POL-lo.

Can I change my order?
Posso cambiare la mia ordinazione?
POS-so kam-bee-A-reh la MEE-a or-dee-na-zee-O-neh?

Do you have a kids menu?
Avete un menu per bambini?
a-VEH-teh oon meh-NOO per bam-BEE-nee?

When does the lunch menu end?
Fino a che ora servite il pranzo?
FEE-no a keh O-ra ser-VEE-teh eel PRAN-zo?

When does the dinner menu start?
Fino a che ora servite la cena?
FEE-no a keh O-ra ser-VEE-teh la CHEH-na?

Do you have any recommendations from the menu?
Ha qualcosa da consigliare* dal menu?
a kwal-KO-sa da kon-seel-lee-A-reh dal meh-NOO?

I would like to place an off-menu order.
Vorrei ordinare qualcosa fuori dal menu.
vor-REH-ee or-dee-NA-reh kwal-KO-sa foo-O-ree dal meh-NOO.

Can we see the dessert menu?
Possiamo vedere il menu dei dolci?
pos-see-A-mo veh-DEH-reh eel meh-NOO DEH-ee DOL-chee?

Is this available sugar free?
È possibile averlo senza zucchero?
EH pos-SEE-bee-leh a-VER-lo SEN-za ZOOK-keh-ro?

May we have the bill, please?
Possiamo avere il conto, per favore?
pos-see-A-mo a-VEH-reh eel KON-to, per fa-VO-reh?

Where do we pay?
Dove paghiamo?
DO-veh pa-ghee-A-mo?

Hi, we are with the party of Isaac.
Salve, siamo col gruppo di Isaac.
SAL-veh, see-A-mo kol GROOP-po dee Isaac.

We haven't made up our minds yet on what to order. Can we have a few more minutes, please?
Non sappiamo ancora cosa ordinare. Possiamo avere un altro paio di minuti, per favore?
non sap-pee-A-mo an-KO-ra KO-sa or-dee-NA-reh. pos-see-A-mo a-VEH-reh oon AL-tro PA-ee-o dee mee-NOO-tee, per fa-VO-reh?

Waiter!
Cameriere!
ka-meh-ree-EH-reh!

Waitress!
Cameriera!
ka-meh-ree-EH-ra!

I'm still deciding, come back to me, please.
Sto ancora scegliendo*, torni tra poco, per favore.
sto an-KO-ra shel-lee-EN-do, TOR-nee tra PO-ko, per fa-VO-reh.

Can we have a pitcher of that?
Possiamo avere una brocca di quello?
pos-see-A-mo a-VEH-reh OO-na BROK-ka dee KWEL-lo?

This is someone else's meal.
Questo è il piatto di qualcun altro.
KWES-to EH eel pee-AT-to dee KWAL-koon AL-tro.

Can you please heat this up a little more?
Potrebbe scaldarlo ancora un po', per favore?
po-TREB-beh skal-DAR-lo an-KO-ra oon PO, per fa-VO-reh?

I'm afraid I didn't order this.
Mi spiace, ma non ho ordinato questo.
mee spee-A-cheh, ma non o or-dee-NA-to KWES-to.

Same again, please.
Mi porti di nuovo lo stesso, per favore.
mee POR-tee dee noo-O-vo lo STES-so, per fa-VO-reh.

Can we have another bottle of wine?
Possiamo avere un'altra bottiglia* di vino?
pos-see-A-mo a-VEH-reh oon-AL-tra bot-TEEL-lee-a dee VEE-no?

That was perfect, thank you!
Era perfetto, grazie!
EH-ra per-FET-to, GRA-zee-eh!

Everything was good.
Era tutto buono.
EH-ra TOOT-to boo-O-no.

Can we have the bill?
Possiamo avere il conto?
pos-see-A-mo a-VEH-reh eel KON-to?

I'm sorry, but this bill is incorrect.
Mi spiace, ma il conto non è corretto.
mee spee-A-cheh, ma eel KON-to non EH kor-RET-to.

Can I have clean cutlery?
Potrei avere delle posate pulite?
po-TREH-ee a-VEH-reh DEL-leh po-SA-teh poo-LEE-teh?

Can we have more napkins?
Potremmo avere altri tovaglioli*?
po-TREM-mo a-VEH-reh AL-tree to-val-lee-O-lee?

May I have another straw?
Posso avere un'altra cannuccia?
POS-so a-VEH-reh oon-AL-tra kan-NOOCH-chee-a?

What sides can I have with that?
Quali contorni posso avere con questo?
KWA-lee kon-TOR-nee POS-so a-VEH-reh kon KWES-to?

Excuse me, but this is overcooked.
Mi scusi, ma è stracotto.
mee SKOO-see, ma EH stra-KOT-to.

May I talk to the chef?
Posso parlare con lo chef?
POS-so par-LA-reh kon lo chef?

We have booked a table for fifteen people.
Abbiamo prenotato un tavolo per 15 persone.
ab-bee-AH-mo preh-no-TA-to oon TA-vo-lo per KWIN-dee-chee per-SO-neh.

Are there any tables free?
Ci sono dei tavoli liberi?
chee SO-no DEH-ee TA-vo-lee LEE-beh-ree?

I would like one beer, please.
Vorrei una birra, per favore.
vor-REH-ee OO-na BEER-ra, per fa-VO-reh.

Can you add ice to this?
Può aggiungere del ghiaccio?
poo-O aj-JOON-jeh-reh del ghee-A-chee-oh?

I would like to order a dark beer.
Vorrei ordinare una birra scura.
vor-REH-ee or-dee-NA-reh OO-na BEER-ra SKOO-ra.

Do you have any beer from the tap?
Avete delle birre alla spina?
a-VEH-teh DEL-leh BEER-reh AL-la SPEE-na?

How expensive is your champagne?
Quanto costa il vostro champagne?
KWAN-to KOS-ta eel VOS-tro SHAM-pan?

Enjoy your meal.
Buon appetito.
boo-ON ap-peh-TEE-to.

I want this.
Voglio* questo.
VOL-lee-o KWES-to.

Please cook my meat well done.
Per favore, faccia la mia carne ben cotta.
per fa-VO-reh, FA-chee-a la MEE-a KAR-neh ben KOT-ta.

Please cook my meat medium rare.
Per favore, faccia la mia carne a cottura media.
per fa-VO-reh, FA-chee-a la MEE-a KAR-neh a kot-TOO-ra MEH-dee-a.

Please prepare my meat rare.
Per favore, faccia la mia carne al sangue.
per fa-VO-reh, FA-chee-a la MEE-a KAR-neh al SAN-goo-eh.

What type of fish do you serve?
Che tipo di pesce servite?
keh TEE-po dee PE-sheh ser-VEE-teh?

Can I make a substitution with my meal?
Posso cambiare la mia pietanza?
POS-so kam-bee-A-reh la MEE-a pee-eh-TAN-za?

Do you have a booster seat for my child?
Avete un seggiolone per mio figlio*?
a-VEH-teh oon sej-jo-LO-ne per MEE-o FEEL-lee-oh?

Call us when you get a table.
Ci chiami quando si libera un tavolo.
chee kee-A-mee KWAN-do see LEE-beh-ra oon TA-vo-lo.

Is this a no smoking area?
Questa è una zona per non fumatori?
KWES-ta EH OO-na ZO-na per non foo-ma-TO-ree?

We would like to be seated in the smoking area.
Vorremmo sederci nell'area fumatori.
vor-REM-mo seh-DER-chee nel-LA-reh-a foo-ma-TO-ree.

This meat tastes funny.

Questa carne ha un sapore insolito.

KWES-ta KAR-neh a oon sa-PO-reh in-SO-lee-to.

More people will be joining us later.

Altre persone ci raggiungeranno più tardi.

AL-treh per-SO-neh chee raj-joon-jeh-RAN-no PEW TAR-dee.

TRANSPORTATION

Where's the train station?
Dov'è la stazione dei treni?
dov-EH la sta-zee-O-neh DEH-ee TREH-nee?

How much does it cost to get to this address?
Quanto costa arrivare a questo indirizzo?
KWAN-to KOS-ta ar-ree-VA-reh a KWES-to in-dee-REEZ-zo?

What type of payment do you accept?
Che tipo di pagamento accettate?
keh TEE-po dee-pa-ga-MEN-to a-CHET-ta-teh?

Do you have first class tickets available?
Ci sono biglietti* di prima classe disponibili?
chee SO-no bee-lee-ET-tee dee PREE-ma KLAS-seh dis-po-NEE-bee-lee?

What platform do I need to be on to catch this train?
Su che binario devo andare per prendere questo treno?
soo keh bee-NA-ree-o DEH-vo an-DA-reh per PREN-deh-reh KWES-to TREH-no?

Are the roads paved in this area?
In questa zona le strade sono asfaltate?
in KWES-ta ZO-na leh STRA-deh SO-no as-fal-TA-teh?

Where are the dirt roads and how do I avoid them?
Dove si trovano le strade sterrate e come le posso evitare?
DO-ve see TRO-va-no leh STRA-deh as-fal-TA-teh eh KO-meh leh POS-so eh-vee-TA-reh?

Are there any potholes I need to avoid?
Ci sono delle gallerie che dovrei evitare?
chee SO-no DEL-le gal-leh-REE-eh keh do-VREH-ee eh-vee-TA-reh?

69

How fast are you going?
A che velocità stai andando?
a KEH veh-lo-chee-TA STA-ee an-DAN-do?

Do I need to put my emergency blinkers on?
Devo azionare le frecce d'emergenza?
DEH-vo a-zee-o-NA-reh leh FRE-cheh deh-mer-JEN-za?

Make sure to use the right turn signals.
Assicurati di segnalare* la svolta a destra.
as-see-KOO-ra-tee dee seh-nee-a-LA-reh la SVOL-ta a DES-tra.

We need a good mechanic.
Abbiamo bisogno* di un buon meccanico.
ab-bee-A-mo bee-SON-nee-o dee oon boo-ON mek-KA-nee-ko.

Can we get a push?
Possiamo darci una mossa?
pos-see-A-mo DAR-chee OO-na MOS-sa?

I have to call the towing company to move my car.
Devo chiamare un carro attrezzi per far rimuovere la mia automobile.
DE-vo kee-a-MA-reh oon KAR-ro at-TREZ-zee per far ree-moo-O-veh-reh la MEE-a a-oo-to-MO-bee-leh.

Make sure to check the battery and spark plugs for any problems.
Assicurati di controllare la batteria e le candele per evitare problemi.
as-see-KOO-ra-tee dee kon-trol-LA-reh la bat-teh-REE-a eh leh kan-DEH-leh per eh-vee-TA-reh prob-LEH-mee.

Check the oil level.
Controlla il livello dell'olio.
kon-trol-LA eel lee-VEL-lo del-LO-lee-o.

I need to notify my insurance company.
Devo avvisare la mia compagnia* di assicurazioni.
DE-vo av-vee-SA-reh la MEE-a kom-pan-NEE-a dee as-see-koo-ra-zee-OH-nee.

When do I pay the taxi driver?
Quando pago il tassista?
KWAN-do PA-go eel tas-SEE-sta?

Please take me to the nearest train station.
Per favore, mi porti alla stazione dei treni più vicina.
per fa-VO-reh, mee POR-tee AL-la sta-zee-O-neh DEH-ee TREH-nee PEW vee-CHEE-na.

How long does it take to get to this address?
Quanto ci vuole per raggiungere questo indirizzo?
KWAN-to chee voo-O-leh per raj-JOON-jeh-reh KWES-to in-dee-REEZ-zo?

Can you stop here, please?
Può fermarsi qui, per favore?
poo-O fer-MAR-see KWEE, per fa-VO-reh?

You can drop me off anywhere around here.
Mi può lasciare qui attorno.
mee poo-O la-shee-A-reh KWEE at-TOR-no.

Is there a charge for extra passengers?
C'è un addebito per un passeggero extra?
CHEH oon ad-DEH-bee-to per oon pas-sej-JEH-ro extra?

What is the condition of the road? Is it safe to travel there?
Com'è la condizione della strada? È sicura per viaggiarci?
kom-EH la kon-dee-zee-O-neh DEL-la STRA-da? EH see-KOO-ra per vee-aj-jee-AR-chee?

Take me to the emergency room.
Mi porti al pronto soccorso.
mee POR-tee al PRON-to sok-KOR-so.

Take me to the embassy.
Mi porti all'ambasciata.
mee POR-tee al-lam-ba-shee-A-ta.

I want to travel around the country.
Vorrei viaggiare per tutto il paese.
vor-REH-ee vee-aj-JA-reh per TOOT-to eel pa-EH-seh.

Is this the right side of the road?
È questo il lato giusto della strada?
EH KWES-to eel LA-to JOOS-to DEL-la STRA-da?

My car broke down, please help!
La mia automobile si è rotta, per favore mi aiuti!
la MEE-a a-oo-to-MO-bee-leh see EH ROT-ta, per fa-VO-reh, mee ah-ee-OO-tee!

Can you help me change my tire?
Mi può aiutare a cambiare le gomme?
mee poo-O ah-ee-oo-TA-reh a kam-bee-A-reh leh GOM-meh?

Where can I get a rental car?
Dove posso prendere un'automobile a noleggio?
DO-veh POS-so PREN-deh-reh oon a-oo-to-MO-bee-leh a no-LEJ-jee-o?

Please take us to the hospital.
Per favore, ci porti all'ospedale.
per fa-VO-reh, chee POR-tee al-los-peh-DA-leh.

Is that the car rental office?
È quello l'ufficio per noleggiare un'automobile?
EH KWEL-lo loof-FEE-chee-o per eel no-lej-jee-A-reh oon a-oo-to-MO-bee-leh??

May I have a price list for your fleet?
Posso avere il listino prezzi della vostra compagnia?
POS-so a-VEH-reh eel lis-TEE-no PREZ-zee DEL-la VOS-tra com-pan-NEE-a??

Can I get insurance on this rental car?
Posso avere l'assicurazione con questa automobile a noleggio?
POS-so a-VEH-reh las-see-koo-ra-zee-O-ne kon KWES-ta a-oo-to-MO-bee-leh a no-LEJ-jee-o?

How much is the car per day?
Quanto costa l'automobile al giorno?
KWAN-to KOS-ta la a-oo-to-MO-bee-leh al jee-OR-no?

How many kilometers can I travel with this car?
Quanti chilometri posso percorrere con questa automobile?
KWAN-tee kee-LO-meh-tree POS-so per-KOR-reh-reh kon KWES-ta a-oo-to-MO-bee-leh?

I would like maps of the region if you have them.
Vorrei delle mappe della regione, se ne avete.
vor-REH-ee DEL-le MAP-peh DEL-la reh-JO-neh seh neh a-VEH-teh.

When I am done with the car where do I return it?
Quando avrò finito di usare la automobile, dove devo riconsegnarla?
KWAN-do a-VRO fee-NEE-to dee oo-SA-reh la a-oo-to-MO-bee-leh, DO-veh DEH-vo REE-kon-seh-nee-AR-la?

Is this a standard or automatic transmission?
Il cambio è manuale o automatico?
eel KAM-bee-o EH ma-noo-A-leh o a-oo-to-MA-tee-ko?

Is this car gas efficient? How many kilometers per liter?
Questa automobile consuma poca benzina? Quanti chilometri fa con un litro?
KWES-ta a-oo-to-MO-bee-lehkon-SOO-ma PO-ka ben-ZEE-na? KWAN-tee kee-LO-meh-tree fa kon oon LEE-tro?

Where is the spare tire stored?
Dove si trova la ruota di scorta?
DO-veh see TRO-va la roo-O-ta dee SKOR-ta?

Are there places around the city that are difficult to drive?
Ci sono dei posti complicati in cui è difficile guidare in città?
chee SO-no DEH-ee POS-tee KOM-plee-KA-tee in KOO-ee EH dif-FEE-chee-leh goo-ee-DA-reh in chit-TA?

At what time of the day is the traffic the worst?
A che ora del giorno il traffico è più intenso?
a keh O-ra del jee-OR-no eel TRAF-fee-ko EH PEW een-TEN-so?

We can't park right here.
Non possiamo parcheggiare qui.
non pos-see-A-mo par-kej-JA-reh KWEE.

What is the speed limit?
Qual è il limite di velocità?
kwal-EH eel LEE-mee-teh dee ve-lo-chee-TA?

Keep the change.
Tenga il resto.
TEN-ga eel RES-to.

Now let's get off here.
Ora andiamocene da qui.
O-ra an-dee-A-mo-cheh-neh da KWEE.

Where is the train station?
Dov'è la stazione dei treni?
dov-EH la sta-zee-O-ne DEH-ee TREH-nee?

Is the bus stop nearby?
La fermata dell'autobus è vicina?
la fer-MA-ta dell-A-oo-to-boos EH vee-CHEE-na?

When does the bus run?
Quando passa il bus?
KWAN-do PAS-sa eel BOOS?

Where do I go to catch a taxi?
Dove devo andare per prendere un taxi?
DO-ve DEH-vo an-DA-reh per PREN-deh-reh oon taxi?

Does the train go to the north station?
Il treno va verso la stazione nord?
eel TREH-no va VER-so la sta-zee-O-ne nord?

Where do I go to purchase tickets?
Dove vado per comprare i biglietti*?
DO-ve VA-do per kom-PRA-reh ee beel-lee-ET-tee?

How much is a ticket to Milan?
Quanto costa un biglietto* per Milano?
KWAN-to KOS-ta oon beel-lee-ET-to per mee-la-no?

What is the next stop along this route?
Qual è la prossima fermata in questo itinerario?
kwal-EH la PROS-see-ma fer-MA-ta in KWES-to ee-tee-neh-RA-ree-o?

Can I have a ticket to Milan?
Posso avere un biglietto* per Milano?
POS-so a-VEH-reh oon beel-lee-ET-to per mee-la-no?

Where is my designated platform?
Dov'è il mio binario?
dov-EH eel MEE-o bee-NA-ree-o?

Where do I place my luggage?
Dove posso mettere il mio bagaglio*?
DO-veh POS-so MET-teh-reh eel MEE-o ba-GAL-lee-o?

Are there any planned closures today?
Ci sono delle chiusure pianificate per oggi?
chee SO-no DEL-leh kee-oo-SOO-reh pee-a-nee-fee-KA-teh per OJ-jee?

Where are the machines that disperse tickets?
Dove sono le macchinette per fare i biglietti*?
DO-ve SO-no leh mak-kee-NET-teh per FA-reh ee beel-lee-ET-tee?

Does this car come with insurance?
Con questa automobile è compresa l'assicurazione?
kon KWES-ta a-oo-to-MO-bee-lehEH kom-PRE-sa l-as-see-koo-ra-zee-OH-neh?

May I have a timetable, please?
Posso avere una tabella oraria, per favore?
POS-so a-VEH-reh OO-na ta-BEL-a o-RA-ree-a, per fa-VO-reh?

How often do trains come to this area?
Ogni* quanto passano i treni in questa zona?
ON-nee KWAN-to PAS-sa-no ee TREH-nee in KWES-ta ZOH-na?

Is the train running late?
Il treno è in ritardo?
eel TREH-no EH in ree-TAR-do?

Has the train been cancelled?
Il treno è stato cancellato?
eel TREH-no EH STA-to kan-chel-LA-to?

Is this seat available?
È libero questo posto?
EH LEE-beh-ro KWES-to POS-to?

Do you mind if I sit here?
Le spiace se mi siedo qui?
leh spee-A-cheh seh mee see-EH-do KWEE?

I've lost my ticket.
Ho perso il mio biglietto*.
o PER-so eel MEE-o beel-lee-ET-to.

Excuse me, this is my stop.
Mi scusi, questa è la mia fermata.
mee SKOO-see, KWES-ta EH la MEE-a fer-MA-ta.

Can you please open the window?
Potrebbe, per favore, aprire la finestra?
po-TREB-beh per fa-VO-reh a-PREE-reh la fee-NES-tra?

Is smoking allowed in the car?
Si può fumare in automobile?
see poo-O foo-MA-reh in a-oo-to-MO-bee-leh?

Keep the change.
Tenga il resto.
TEN-ga eel RES-to.

Wait, my luggage is still onboard!
Aspetti, il mio bagaglio* è ancora a bordo!
as-PET-tee, eel MEE-o ba-GAL-lee-o EH an-KO-ra a BOR-do!

Where can I get a map?
Dove posso ottenere una cartina?
DO-veh POS-so ot-teh-NEH-reh OO-na kar-TEE-na?

What zone is this?
Che zona è questa?
keh ZO-na EH KWES-ta?

Please be careful of the gap!
Per favore, stai attento al buco!
per fa-VO-reh, STA-ee at-TEN-to al BOO-ko!

I am about to run out of gas.
Sto per finire la benzina.
sto per fee-NEE-reh la ben-ZEE-na.

My tank is halfway full.
Il mio serbatoio è mezzo pieno.
eel MEE-o ser-ba-TO-ee-o EH MEZ-zo pee-EH-no.

What type of gas does this car take?
Che tipo di benzina ci vuole per questa automobile?
keh TEE-po dee ben-ZEE-na chee voo-O-leh per KWES-ta a-oo-to-MO-bee-leh?

There is gas leaking out of my car.
La mia automobile perde benzina.
la MEE-a a-oo-to-MO-bee-leh PER-deh ben-ZEE-na.

Fill up the tank.
Riempi il serbatoio.
ree-EM-pee eel ser-ba-TO-ee-o.

There is no more gas in my car.
Non c'è più benzina nella mia automobile.
non CHEH PEW ben-ZEE-na NEL-la MEE-a a-oo-to-MO-bee-leh.

Where can I find the nearest gas station?
Dov'è il benzinaio più vicino?
do-VEH eel ben-zee-NA-ee-o PEW vee-CHEE-no?

The engine light for my car is on.
Si è accesa la spia del motore.
see EH a-CHEH-sa la SPEE-a del mo-TO-reh.

Do you mind if I drive?
Ti spiace se guido io?
tee spee-A-cheh seh goo-EE-do EE-o?

Please get in the back seat.
Per favore, sali dietro.
per fa-VO-reh, SA-lee dee-EH-tro.

Let me get my bags out before you leave.
Lascia che prenda le mie borse prima che tu parta.
LA-shee-a keh PREN-da leh MEE-eh BOR-seh PREE-ma keh too PAR-ta.

The weather is bad, please drive slowly.
Il tempo è brutto, vai piano, per favore.
eel TEM-po EH BROOT-to, VA-ee pee-A-no, per fa-VO-reh.

Our vehicle isn't equipped to travel there.
Il nostro veicolo non è equipaggiato per viaggiare qui.
eel NOS-tro veh-EE-ko-lo non EH eh-kwee-paj-JA-to per vee-aj-JA-reh KWEE.

One ticket to Milan, please.
Un biglietto* per Milano per favore.
oon beel-lee-ET-to per mee-la-no per fa-VO-reh.

If you get lost, call me.
Se ti perdi, chiamami.
seh tee PER-dee, kee-A-ma-mee.

That bus is overcrowded. I will wait for the next one.
Il bus è affollato. Aspetterò il prossimo.
eel boos EH af-fol-LA-to. as-pet-teh-RO eel PROS-see-mo.

Please, take my seat.
Prego, le lascio il posto.
PREH-go, leh LA-shee-o eel POS-to.

Ma'am, I think your stop is coming up.
Signora*, penso sia la sua fermata.
seen-nee-O-ra, PEN-so SEE-a la SOO-a fer-MA-ta.

Wake me up when we get to our destination.
Svegliami* quando arriveremo a destinazione.
SVEL-lee-a-mee KWAN-do ar-ree-VEH-re-mo a des-tee-na-zee-O-neh.

I would like to purchase a travel pass for the entire day.
Vorrei acquistare un biglietto* valido per tutto il giorno.
vor-REH-ee a-kwis-TA-reh oon beel-lee-ET-to VA-lee-do per TOOT-to eel jee-OR-no.

Would you like to swap seats with me?
Le spiace cambiare posto col mio?
leh spee-A-cheh kam-bee-A-reh POS-to kol MEE-o?

I want to sit with my family.
Vorrei sedermi con la mia famiglia*.
vor-REH-ee seh-DER-mee kon la MEE-a fa-MEEL-lee-a.

I would like a window seat for this trip.
Vorrei un posto vicino al finestrino per questo viaggio.
vor-REH-ee oon POS-to vee-CHEE-no al fee-nes-TREE-no per KWES-to vee-AJ-jee-o.

RELIGIOUS QUESTIONS

Where can I go to pray?
Dove posso andare per pregare?
DO-veh POS-so an-DA-reh per preh-GA-reh?

What services does your church offer?
Che servizi offre la vostra chiesa?
keh ser-VEE-zee OF-freh la VOS-tra kee-EH-sa?

Are you non-denominational?
Siete laici?
see-EH-teh lie-chee?

Is there a shuttle to your church?
C'è una navetta per la vostra chiesa?
CHEH OO-na na-VET-ta per la VOS-tra kee-EH-sa?

How long does church last?
Quanto dura la messa?
KWAN-to DOO-ra la MES-sa?

Where is your bathroom?
Dov'è il bagno*?
dov-EH eel BAN-nee-o?

What should I wear to your services?
Cosa devo indossare durante la messa?
KO-sa DEH-vo in-dos-SA-reh doo-RAN-teh la MES-sa?

Where is the nearest Catholic Church?
Dov'è la chiesa cattolica più vicina?
do-VEH la kee-EH-sa kat-TO-lee-ka PEW vee-CHEE-na?

Where is the nearest Mosque?
Dov'è la moschea più vicina?
do-VEH la mos-KEH-a PEW vee-CHEE-na?

Does your church perform weddings?
La vostra chiesa celebra anche matrimoni?
la VOS-tra kee-EH-sa CHEH-leh-bra AN-keh ma-tree-MO-nee?

Who is getting married?
Chi si sposa?
kee see SPO-sa?

Will our marriage license be legal if we leave the country?
La nostra licenza matrimoniale è legale se lasciamo il paese?
la NOS-tra lee-CHEN-za ma-tree-mo-nee-A-leh EH leh-GA-leh seh la-SHEE-a-mo EEL pa-EH-seh?

Where do we get our marriage license?
Dove possiamo ottenere la licenza di matrimonio?
DO-veh pos-see-A-mo ot-teh-NEH-reh la lee-CHEN-za dee ma-tree-MO-nee-o?

What is the charge for marrying us?
A quanto ammonta la tassa per il matrimonio?
a KWAN-to am-MON-ta la TAS-sa per eel ma-tree-MO-nee-o?

Do you handle same sex marriage?
Celebrate anche matrimoni dello stesso sesso?
CHEH-leh-BRA-teh AN-keh ma-tree-MO-nee DEL-lo STES-so SES-so?

Please gather here to pray.
Per favore, raccoglietevi* qui per pregare.
per fa-VO-reh, rak-kol-lee-EH-teh-vee KWEE per pre-GA-reh.

I would like to lead a sermon.
Vorrei condurre il sermone.
vor-REH-ee kon-DOOR-reh eel ser-MO-meh.

I would like to help with prayer.
Vorrei aiutare durante la preghiera.
vor-REH-ee a-ee-oo-TA-reh doo-RAN-teh la preh-ghee-EH-ra.

How should I dress before arriving?
Come mi devo vestire prima di arrivare?
KO-meh mee DEH-vo ves-TEE-reh PREE-ma dee ar-ree-VA-reh?

What are your rules?
Quali sono le regole?
KWA-lee SO-no leh REH-go-leh?

Are cell phones allowed in your building?
I cellulari sono permessi nell'edificio?
ee chel-loo-LA-ree SO-no per-MES-see nel-leh-dee-FEE-chee-o?

I plan on bringing my family this Sunday.
Credo che porterò la mia famiglia* questa domenica.
KREH-do KEH por-teh-RO la MEE-a fa-MEEL-lee-a KWES-ta do-MEH-nee-ka.

Do you accept donations?
Accettate donazioni?
a-chet-TA-teh do-na-zee-O-nee?

I would like to offer my time to your cause.
Vorrei offrire il mio tempo per la vostra causa.
vor-REH-ee of-FREE-reh eel MEE-o TEM-po per la VOS-tra KA-oo-sa.

What book should I be reading from?
Da quale libro dovrei leggere?
da KWA-leh LEE-bro do-VREH-ee LEJ-jeh-reh?

Do you have a gift store?
Avete un negozio di souvenir?
a-VEH-teh oon ne-GO-zee-o dee souvenir?

EMERGENCY

I need help over here!
Ho bisogno* di aiuto qui!
o bee-SON-nee-o dee a-ee-OO-to KWEE!

I'm lost, please help me.
Mi sono perso, per favore, mi aiuti.
mee SO-no PER-so, per fa-VO-reh, mee a-ee-OO-tee.

Someone call the police!
Qualcuno chiami la polizia!
kwal-KOO-no kee-A-mee la po-lee-ZEE-a!

Is there a lawyer who speaks English?
C'è un avvocato che parli inglese?
cheh oon av-vo-KA-to keh PAR-lee in-GLEH-seh?

Please help, my car doesn't work.
Per favore, mi aiuti, la mia automobile non va.
per fa-VO-reh, mee a-ee-OO-tee, la MEE-a a-oo-to-MO-bee-leh non va.

There was a collision!
C'è stato uno scontro!
cheh STA-to OO-no SKON-tro!

Call an ambulance!
Chiama un'ambulanza!
kee-A-ma oo-nam-boo-LAN-za!

Am I under arrest?
Sono in arresto?
SO-no in ar-RES-to?

I need an interpreter, this is an emergency!
Ho bisogno* di un interprete, è un'emergenza!
o bee-SON-nee-o dee OON in-TER-preh-teh, EH oon-eh-mer-JEN-za!

My back hurts.
Mi fa male la schiena.
mee fa MA-leh la skee-EH-na.

Is there an American consulate here?
C'è un consolato Americano qui?
CHEH oon kon-so-LA-to a-meh-ree-KA-no KWEE?

I'm sick and don't feel too well.
Sono malato e non mi sento troppo bene.
SO-no ma-LA-to eh non mee SEN-to TROP-po BEH-neh.

Is there a pharmacy where I can get medicine?
C'è una farmacia dove poter acquistare delle medicine?
CHEH OO-na far-ma-CHEE-a DO-veh po-TER ak-kwis-TA-reh DEL-leh meh-dee-CHEE-neh?

I need a doctor immediately.
Ho bisogno* immediatamente di un dottore.
o bee-SON-nee-o im-meh-dee-a-ta-MEN-teh dee oon dot-TO-reh.

I have a tooth missing.
Ho perso un dente.
o PER-so oon DEN-teh.

Please! Someone bring my child to me!
Per favore! Qualcuno mi porti mio figlio*!
Per fa-VO-reh, kwal-KOO-no mee POR-tee MEE-o FEE-lee-o!

Where does it hurt?
Dove le fa male?
DO-veh tee fa MA-leh?

Hold on to me!
Aggrappati a me!
ag-GRAP-pa-tee a meh!

There's an emergency!
C'è un'emergenza!
CHEH oon-eh-mer-JEN-za!

I need a telephone to call for help.
Ho bisogno* di un telefono per chiedere aiuto.
o bee-SO-nee-o dee oon teh-LEH-fo-no per kee-EH-deh-reh a-ee-OO-to.

My nose is bleeding.
Il mio naso sta sanguinando.
eel MEE-o NA-so sta san-goo-ee-NAN-do.

I twisted my ankle.
Ho preso una storta alla caviglia*.
o PREH-so OO-na STOR-ta AL-la ka-VEEL-lee-a.

I don't feel so good.
Non mi sento molto bene.
non mee SEN-to MOL-to BEH-neh.

Don't move, please.
Non ti muovere, per favore.
non tee moo-O-veh-re, per fa-VO-reh.

Hello operator, can I place a collect call?
Salve operatore, posso fare una chiamata a carico del destinatario?
SAL-veh o-peh-ra-TO-reh, POS-so FA-reh OO-na kee-a-MA-ta a KA-ree-ko del des-tee-na-TA-ree-o?

I'll get a doctor for you.
Ti chiamerò un dottore.
tee kee-a-meh-RO oon dot-TO-reh.

Please hold my passports for a while.
Per favore, tienimi il passaporto per un po'.
per fa-VO-reh, tee-EH-nee-mee eel pas-sa-POR-to per oon PO.

I lost my wallet.
Ho perso il mio portafogli*.
o PER-so eel MEE-o por-ta-FOL-lee.

I have a condition! Please check my wallet.
Ho una patologia! Per favore, controlla il mio portafogli*.
o OO-na pa-to-lo-JEE-a! per fa-VO-reh, kon-TROL-la eel MEE-o por-ta-FOL-lee.

My wife is in labor please help!
Mia moglie* è in travaglio*, per favore, aiuto!
MEE-a MO-lee-eh EH in tra-VAL-lee-o, per fa-VO-reh, a-ee-OO-to!

I would like to talk to my lawyer.
Vorrei parlare con il mio avvocato.
vor-REH-ee par-LA-reh con eel MEE-o av-vo-KA-to.

It's an earthquake!
È un terremoto.
EH oon ter-reh-MO-to.

Get under the desk and protect your head.
Mettiti sotto il tavolo e proteggiti la testa.
MET-tee-tee SOT-to eel TA-vo-lo eh pro-TEJ-jee-tee la TES-ta.

How can I help you?
Come posso aiutarla?
KO-meh POS-so a-ee-oo-TAR-la?

Everyone, he needs help!
Ascoltate tutti, ha bisogno* di aiuto!
as-kol-TA-teh TOOT-tee, a bee-SON-nee-o dee a-ee-OO-to!

Yes, help me get an ambulance.
Sì, mi aiuti a chiamare un'ambulanza.
see, mee a-ee-OO-tee a kee-a-MA-reh oon-am-boo-LAN-za.

Thank you, but I am fine. Please don't help me.
Grazie, sto bene. Per favore, non mi aiuti.
GRA-zee-eh, sto BEH-neh. per fa-VO-reh, non mee a-ee-OO-tee.

I need help carrying this injured person.
Ho bisogno* di aiuto per trasportare questa persona ferita.
o bee-SON-nee-o dee a-ee-OO-to per tras-por-TA-reh KWES-ta per-SO-na feh-REE-ta.

TECHNOLOGY

What is the country's official website?
Qual è la pagina web ufficiale del paese?
kwal-EH la PA-jee-na oof-fee-chee-A-leh del pa-EH-seh?

Do you know the name of a good wi-fi café?
Sai dirmi il nome di un buon bar con servizio wi-fi?
SA-ee DEER-mee il NO-meh dee oon boo-ON bar kon ser-VEE-zee-o wi-fi?

Do you have any experience with computers?
Hai esperienza coi computer?
A-ee es-peh-ree-EN-za KO-ee computer?

How well do you know Apple products?
Quanto bene conosci i prodotti Apple?
KWAN-to BEH-neh ko-NO-shee ee pro-DOT-tee Apple?

What kind of work did you do with computers?
Che tipo di lavoro fai coi computer?
keh TEE-po dee la-VO-ro FA-ee KO-ee computer?

Are you a programmer?
Sei un programmatore?
SEH-ee oon pro-gram-ma-TO-reh?

Are you a developer?
Sei uno sviluppatore?
SEH-ee OO-no svee-loop-pa-TO-reh?

I want to use that computer instead of that one.
Voglio* usare quel computer al posto di questo.
VOL-lee-o oo-SA-reh KWEL computer al POS-to dee KWES-to.

Do you know where I can buy discount computer parts?
Sai dove posso comprare dei ricambi per computer a basso prezzo?
SA-ee DO-ve POS-so kom-PRA-reh DEH-ee ree-KAM-bee per computer a BAS-so PREZ-zo?

I have ten years' experience with Windows.
Ho dieci anni di esperienza con Windows.
O dee-EH-chee AN-nee dee es-peh-ree-EN-za kon Windows.

What is the wi-fi password?
Qual è la password del wi-fi?
kwal-EH la password del wi-fi?

I need to have my login information reset.
Ho bisogno* di resettare le informazioni di login.
O bee-SON-nee-o dee re-set-TA-re le een-for-ma-zee-O-nee dee login.

The hard drive is making a clicking noise.
L'hard disk emette un ticchettio.
LARD disk eh-MET-teh oon teek-ket-TEE-o.

How do I uninstall this program from my device?
Come disinstallo questo programma dal mio dispositivo?
KO-me dee-seen-STAL-lo KWES-to pro-GRAM-ma dal MEE-o dis-po-see-TEE-vo?

Can you help me set up a new account with this website?
Puoi aiutarmi a creare un nuovo account per questo sito web?
poo-O-ee a-ee-oo-TAR-mee a kreh-A-reh oon noo-O-vo account per KWES-to SEE-to web?

Why is the internet so slow?
Perché internet è così lento?
per-KEH internet EH ko-SEE LEN-to?

Why is YouTube buffering every video I play?
Perché c'è il buffering su YouTube qualsiasi video riproduca?
per-KEH CHEH eel buffering soo YouTube kwal-see-A-see video ree-PRO-doo-ka?

My web camera isn't displaying a picture.
La mia webcam non mostra alcuna immagine.
la MEE-a webcam non MOS-tra al-KOO-na EM-maj-jee-neh.

I have no bars on my phone.
Il cellulare non prende.
eel chel-loo-LA-reh non PREN-deh.

Where can I get my phone serviced?
Dove posso fare aggiustare il mio telefono?
DO-veh POS-so FA-reh aj-joos-TA-re eel MEE-o teh-LEH-fo-no?

My phone shows that it is charging but won't charge.
Il mio telefono indica che si sta caricando, ma non lo sta facendo.
*eel MEE-o teh-LEH-fo-no IN-dee-ka keh see STA ka-ree-KAN-do, ma non lo
STA fa-CHEN-do.*

I think someone else is controlling my computer.
Credo che qualcuno stia controllando il mio computer.
KREH-do keh kwal-KOO-no STEE-a kon-trol-LAN-do eel MEE-o computer.

My computer just gave a blue screen and shut down.
Sul mio computer è comparsa una schermata blu e si è spento.
*sool MEE-o computer EH kom-PAR-sa OO-na sker-MA-ta bloo eh see EH
SPEN-to.*

Do you have the battery for this laptop?
Ha una batteria per questo laptop?
a OO-na bat-teh-REE-a per KWES-to laptop?

Where can I get a compatible adapter?
Dove posso acquistare un adattatore compatibile?
DO-ve POS-so ak-kwees-TA-reh oon a-dat-ta-TO-reh kom-pa-TEE-bee-leh?

I can't get online with the information you gave me.
Non riesco a connettermi con le informazioni che mi hai dato.
*non ree-ES-ko a kon-NET-ter-mee kon leh in-for-ma-zee-O-nee keh mee A-
ee DA-to.*

This keyboard is not working correctly.
Questa tastiera non funziona correttamente.
KWES-ta tas-tee-EH-ra non foon-zee-O-na kor-ret-ta-MEN-teh.

What is the login information for this computer?
Quali sono le informazioni di login per questo computer?
KWA-lee SO-no leh in-for-ma-zee-O-nee dee login per KWES-to computer?

I need you to update my computer.
Ho bisogno* di te per aggiornare il computer.
O bee-SON-nee-o dee teh per aj-jor-NA-reh eel computer.

Can you build my website?
Puoi creare il mio sito web?
poo-O-ee kreh-A-reh eel MEE-o SEE-to web?

I would prefer Wordpress.
Preferirei Wordpress.
preh-feh-ree-REH-ee Wordpress.

What are your rates per hour?
Qual è la tua tariffa oraria?
kwal-EH la TOO-a ta-REEF-fa o-RA-ree-a?

Do you have experience handling email servers?
Hai esperienza con i server email?
A-ee es-peh-ree-EN-za kon ee server email?

I am locked out of my account, can you help?
Non riesco ad accedere al mio account, mi puoi aiutare?
non ree-ES-ko ad a-CHEH-deh-reh al MEE-o account, mee poo-O-ee a-ee-oo-TA-reh?

None of the emails I am sending are going through.
Nessuna delle mail che mando va a destinazione.
nes-SOO-na DEL-le email keh MAN-do va a des-tee-na-zee-O-neh.

The time and date on my computer is wrong.
L'ora e la data sul mio computer sono sbagliate*.
LO-ra eh la DA-ta sool MEE-o computer SO-no sbal-lee-A-teh.

Is this game free to play?
Questo gioco è gratuito?
KWES-to jee-O-ko EH gra-TOO-ee-to?

Where do I go to download the client?
Dove posso scaricare il client?
DO-ve POS-so ska-ree-KA-reh eel client?

I am having troubles chatting with my family.
Ho problemi a chattare con la mia famiglia*.
O pro-BLEH-mee a chat-TA-reh kon la MEE-a fa-MEEL-lee-a.

Is this the fastest computer here?
È questo il computer più veloce qui?
EH KWES-to eel computer PEW veh-LO-cheh KWEE?

How much space is on the computer?
Quanto spazio c'è su questo computer?
KWAN-to SPA-zee-o CHEH soo KWES-to computer?

Will my profile be deleted once I log out? Or does it save?
Il mio profilo sarà cancellato una volta uscito? O sarà salvato?
eel MEE-o pro-FEE-lo sa-RA kan-chel-LA-to OO-na VOL-ta oo-SHEE-to? o sa-RA sal-VA-to?

How much do you charge for computer use?
Quanto vuole per l'uso del computer?
KWAN-to voo-O-leh per LOO-so del computer?

Are group discounts offered?
Vengono offerti sconti di gruppo?
VEN-go-no of-FER-tee SKON-tee dee GROOP-po?

Can I use my own headphones with your computer?
Posso usare le mie cuffie con questo computer?
POS-so oo-SA-reh leh MEE-eh KOOF-fee-eh kon KWES-to computer?

Do you have a data cap?
Avete un limite di traffico dati?
a-VEH-teh oon LEE-mee-teh dee TRAF-fee-ko DA-tee?

I think this computer has a virus.
Credo che questo computer abbia un virus.
KREH-do keh KWES-to computer AB-bee-a oon VEE-roos.

The battery for my laptop is running low.
La batteria del mio laptop si sta scaricando.
la bat-teh-REE-a del MEE-o laptop see STA ska-ree-KAN-do.

Where can I plug this in? I need to recharge my device.
Dove posso collegarlo? Dovrei ricaricare il mio dispositivo.
DO-veh POS-so kol-leh-GAR-lo? do-VREH-ee ree-ka-ree-KA-reh eel MEE-o dis-po-see-TEE-vo.

Do you have a mini usb cord?
Hai un cavo mini usb?
A-ee oon KA-vo mini usb?

Where can I go to watch the game?
Dove posso andare per vedere la partita?
DO-veh POS-so an-DA-reh per veh-DEH-reh la par-TEE-ta?

Do you have an iPhone charger?
Hai un carica batterie per l'iPhone?
A-ee oon KA-ree-ka bat-teh-REE-eh per la-ee-FON?

I need a new battery for my watch.
Ho bisogno* di una nuova batteria per il mio orologio.
o bee-SON-nee-o dee OO-na noo-O-va bat-teh-REE-a per eel MEE-o o-ro-LO-jee-o.

I need to borrow an HDMI cord.
Devo farmi prestare un cavo HDMI.
DEH-vo FAR-mee pres-TA-reh oon KA-vo HDMI.

What happens when I exceed the data cap?
Cosa succede se supero il limite del traffico dei dati?
KO-sa soo-CHEH-deh seh SOO-peh-ro eel LEE-mee-teh del TRAF-fee-ko DEH-ee DA-tee?

Can you help me pair my Bluetooth device?
Può aiutarmi a connettere il mio dispositivo Bluetooth?
poo-O a-ee-oo-TAR-mee a kon-NET-teh-reh eel MEE-o dis-po-see-TEE-vo Bluetooth?

I need a longer ethernet cord.
Ho bisogno* di un cavo Ethernet più lungo.
o bee-SON-nee-o dee oon KA-vo Ethernet PEW LOON-go.

Why is this website restricted?
Perché questo sito web è ad accesso limitato?
per-KEH KWES-to SEE-to web EH ad a-CHES-so lee-mee-TA-to?

How can I unblock this website?
Come posso sbloccare il sito web?
KO-me POS-so blok-KA-reh eel SEE-to web?

Is that television 4k or higher?
Questo televisore è 4k o superiore?
KWES-to teh-leh-vee-SO-re EH KWAT-tro KAP-pa o soo-peh-ree-O-reh?

Do you have the office suite on this computer?
Office è installato su questo computer?
Office EH in-stal-LA-to soo KWES-to computer?

This application won't install on my device.
Questa applicazione non si installerà sul mio dispositivo.
KWES-ta ap-plee-ka-zee-O-neh non see in-stal-leh-RA sool MEE-o dis-po-see-TEE-vo.

Can you change the channel on the television?
Puoi cambiare canale del televisore?
poo-O-ee kam-bee-A-reh ka-NA-leh del teh-le-vee-SO-reh?

I think a fuse blew.
Penso sia saltato un fusibile.
PEN-so SEE-a sal-TA-to oon foo-SEE-bee-leh.

The screen is black and won't come on.
Lo schermo è nero e non si riaccende.
lo SKER-mo EH NEH-ro e non see ree-a-CHEN-deh.

I keep getting popups on every website.
Continuo a vedere popup su ogni* sito web.
kon-TEE-noo-o a veh-DEH-reh popup soo ON-nee SEE-to web.

This computer is moving much slower than it should.
Questo computer è molto più lento di quello che dovrebbe.
KWES-to computer EH MOL-to PEW LEN-to dee KWEL-lo keh do-VREB-beh .

I need to reactivate my copy of Windows.
Devo riattivare la mia copia di Windows.
DE-vo ree-at-tee-VA-reh la MEE-a KO-pee-a dee Windows.

Why is this website blocked on my laptop?
Perché questo sito web è bloccato sul mio laptop?
per-KEH KWES-to SEE-to web EH blok-KA-to sool MEE-o laptop?

Can you show me how to download videos to my computer?
Puoi mostrarmi come scaricare video sul mio computer?
poo-O-ee mos-TRAR-mee KO-me ska-ree-KA-reh video sool MEE-o computer?

Can I insert a flash drive into this computer?
Posso inserire una chiavetta USB in questo computer?
POS-so in-seh-REE-reh OO-na kee-a-VET-ta USB in KWES-to computer?

I want to change computers.
Voglio* cambiare computer.
vo- lee-o -ee kam-bee-A-reh computer.

Is Chrome the only browser I can use with this computer?
Chrome è l'unico browser che posso usare su questo computer?
Chrome EH LOO-nee-ko browser keh POS-so oo-SA-reh soo KWES-to computer?

Do you track my usage on any of these devices?
le mie attività vengono registrate su qualcuno di questi dispositivi?
leh MEE-eh at-tee-vee-TA VEN-go-no reh-gees-TRA-teh soo kwal-KOO-no dee KWES-tee dis-po-see-TEE-vee?

CONVERSATION TIPS

Pardon me.
Mi scusi.
mee SKOO-see

Please speak more slowly.
Per favore, può parlare più lentamente.
per fa-VO-reh, poo-O par-LA-reh PEW len-ta-MEN-teh?

I don't understand.
Non capisco.
non ka-PEES-ko.

Can you say that more clearly?
Può dirlo di nuovo più chiaramente?
poo-O DEER-lo dee noo-O-vo PEW kee-a-ra-MEN-teh?

I don't speak Spanish very well.
Non parlo molto bene lo spagnolo*.
non PAR-lo MOL-to BEH-neh lo span-nee-O-lo.

Can you please translate that to English for me?
Puoi tradurlo in inglese per me, per favore?
poo-O-ee tra-DOOR-lo in in-GLEH-seh per meh, per fa-VO-reh?

Let's talk over there where it is quieter.
Parliamone lì, che è più tranquillo.
par-lee-A-mo-neh lee, keh EH PEW tran-KWIL-lo.

Sit down over there.
Siediti lì.
see-EH-dee-tee lee.

May I?
Posso?
POS-so?

I am from America.
Sono americano.
SO-no a-meh-ree-KA-no.

Am I talking too much?
Sto parlando troppo?
sto par-LAN-do TROP-po?

I speak your language badly.
Parlo male la tua lingua.
PAR-lo MA-leh la TOO-a LIN-goo-a.

Am I saying that word correctly?
Sto pronunciando correttamente questa parola?
sto pro-noon-chee-AN-do cor-ret-ta-MEN-te la TOO-a LIN-goo-A?

You speak English very well.
Parli inglese molto bene.
PAR-lee in-GLEH-seh MOL-to BE-neh.

This is my first time in your lovely country.
È la mia prima volta nel tuo incantevole paese.
EH la MEE-a PREE-ma VOL-ta nel TOO-o in-kan-teh-voo-leh pa-EH-seh.

Write that information down on this piece of paper.
Scrivi quell'informazione su un pezzo di carta.
SKREE-vee KWEL in-for-ma-zee-O-neh soo oon PEZ-zo dee KAR-ta.

Do you understand?
Capisci?
ka-PEE-shee?

How do you pronounce that word?
Come pronunci questa parola?
KO-meh pro-NOON-chee KWES-ta pa-RO-la?

Is this how you write this word?
È così che si scrive questa parola?
EH ko-SEE keh see SKREE-veh KWES-ta pa-RO-la?

Can you give me an example?
Mi puoi fare un esempio?
mee poo-O-ee FA-reh oon eh-SEM-pee-o?

Wait a moment, please.
Aspetta un attimo, per favore.
as-PET-ta oon AT-tee-mo, per fa-VO-reh.

If there is anything you want, tell me.
Se vuoi qualcosa, dimmelo.
SEH voo-O-ee KWAL-ko-sa, DIM-meh-lo.

I don't want to bother you anymore, so I will go.
Non voglio* più darti fastidio, così me ne andrò.
non VOL-lee-o PEW DAR-tee fas-TEE-dee-o, ko-SEE meh neh an-DRO.

Please take care of yourself.
Abbi cura di te.
AB-bee KOO-ra dee TEH.

When you arrive, let us know.
Facci sapere quando arrivi.
FA-chee sa-PEH-re KWAN-do ar-REE-vee.

DATE NIGHT

What is your telephone number?
Qual è il tuo numero di telefono?
KWAL-eh eel TOO-o NOO-meh-ro dee teh-LEH-fo-no?

I'll call you for the next date.
Ti chiamerò per un altro appuntamento.
tee kee-a-meh-RO per oon AL-tro ap-poon-ta-MEN-to.

I had a good time, can't wait to see you again.
Mi sono trovato bene, non vedo l'ora di rivederti .
mee SO-no tro-VA-to BEH-neh, non VEH-do LO-ra dee ree-veh-DER-tee .

I'll pay for dinner tonight.
Offro io la cena questa sera.
OF-fro EE-o la CHEH-na KWES-ta SEH-ra.

Dinner at my place?
Vieni a cena da me?
vee-EH-nee a CHEH-na da MEH?

I don't think we should see each other anymore.
Credo che non dovremmo più vederci..
KREH-do keh non do-VREM-mo PEW veh-DER-chee .

I'm afraid this will be the last time we see each other.
Mi spiace, ma questa sarà l'ultima volta che ci vediamo.
mee spee-A-cheh ma KWES-ta sa-RA LOOL-tee-ma VOL-ta keh chee veh-dee-A-mo.

You look fantastic.
Stai benissimo.
STA-ee beh-NEES-see-mo.

Would you like to dance with me?
Vuoi ballare con me?
voo-O-ee bal-LA-reh kon MEH?

Are there any 3D cinemas in this city?
Ci sono cinema 3D in questa città?
chee SO-no CHEE-neh-ma in KWES-ta chit-TA?

We should walk along the beach.
Dovremmo camminare lungo la spiaggia.
do-VREM-mo kam-mee-NA-reh LOON-go la spee-AJ-jee-a.

I hope you like my car.
Spero ti piaccia la mia macchina.
SPEH-ro tee pee-A-chee-a la MEE-a MAK-kee-na.

What movies are playing today?
Quali film proiettano oggi?
kwa-lee film pro-YET-tah-noo OJ-jee?

I've seen this film but I wouldn't mind watching it again.
Ho già visto questo film, ma lo riguardo volentieri.
o jee-A VIS-to KWES-to fim, ma lo ree-GWAR-do vo-len-tee-EH-ree.

Do you know how to do the salsa?
Sai ballare la salsa?
SA-ee bal-LA-reh la SAL-sa?

We can dance all night.
Possiamo ballare tutta la notte.
pos-see-A-mo bal-LA-reh TOOT-ta la NOT-teh.

I have some friends that will be joining us tonight.
Questa sera alcuni amici si uniranno a noi .
KWES-ta SEH-ra al-KOO-nee a-MEE-chee see oo-nee-RAN-no a NO-ee .

Is this a musical or a regular concert?
È un musical o un concerto normale?
EH oon musical o oon kon-CHER-to nor-MA-leh?

Did you get VIP tickets?
Avevi dei biglietti* VIP?
a-VEH-vee DEH-ee beel-lee-ET-tee VEEP?

I'm going to have to cancel on you tonight. Maybe another time?
Purtroppo devo annullare l'incontro di stasera. Potremmo fare un'altra volta?
poor-TROP-po DEH-vo an-nool-LA-reh leen-KON-tro dee sta-SEH-ra. po-TREM-mo FA-reh oon-AL-tra VOL-ta?

If you want, we can go to your place.
Se vuoi, possiamo andare da te.
seh voo-O-ee pos-see-A-mo an-DA-reh da TEH.

I'll pick you up tonight.
Ti verrò a prendere io stasera.
tee VEHR-roo a PREN-deh-reh ee-O sta-SEH-ra.

This one is for you!
Questo è per te!
KWES-to EH per TEH!

What time does the party start?
A che ora inizia la festa?
a keh O-ra ee-NEE-zee-a la FES-ta?

Will it end on time or will you have to leave early?
Finirà in tempo o te ne dovrai andare prima?
fee-nee-RA in TEM-po o teh neh do-VRA-ee an-DA-reh PREE-ma?

Did you like your gift?
Ti piace il regalo?
tee pee-A-cheh eel reh-GA-lo?

I want to invite you to watch a movie with me tonight.
Questa sera Vorrei invitarti a vedere un film .
KWES-ta SEH-ra vor-REH-ee in-vee-TAR-tee a veh-DEH-reh oon film .

Do you want anything to drink?
Vuoi qualcosa da bere?
voo-O-ee KWAL-ko-sa da BEH-reh?

I am twenty-six years old.
Ho ventisei anni.
o ven-tee-SEH-ee AN-nee.

You're invited to a small party I'm having at my house.
Sei invitata ad una piccola festa che farò a casa mia.
SEH-ee in-vee-TA-ta ad OO-na PEEK-ko-la FES-ta keh fa-RO a KA-sa MEE-a.

I love you.
Ti voglio* bene. / Ti amo.
TEE VOL-lee-o BEH-neh. / TEE A-mo.

We should go to the arcade.
Dovremmo andare in sala giochi.
do-VREM-mo an-DA-reh in SA-la jee-O-kee.

Have you ever played this game before?
Hai mai giocato a questo gioco prima?
A-ee MA-ee jee-o-KA-to a KWES-to jee-O-ko PREE-ma?

Going on this ferry would be really romantic.
Sarebbe romantico andare su questo traghetto.
sa-REB-beh ro-MAN-tee-ko an-DA-reh soo KWES-to tra-GET-to.

How about a candlelight dinner?
Che ne dici di una cena a lume di candela?
keh neh DEE-chee dee OO-na CHEH-na a LOO-me dee kan-DEH-la?

Let's dance and sing!
Balliamo e cantiamo!
bal-lee-A-mo eh kan-tee-A-mo!

Will you marry me?
Mi vuoi sposare?
mee voo-O-ee spo-SA-reh?

Set the table, please.
Prepara la tavola, per favore.
preh-PA-ra la TA-vo-la, per fa-VO-reh.

Here the dishes and the glasses.
Ecco i piatti e i bicchieri.
EK-ko ee pee-AT-tee eh ee beek-kee-EH-ree.

Where is the cutlery?
Dove sono le posate?
DO-ve SO-no leh po-SA-teh?

May I hold your hand?
Posso tenerti la mano?
POS-so teh-NER-tee la MA-no?

Let me get that for you.
Lascia che lo prenda per te.
LA-shee-a keh lo PREN-da per teh.

I think our song is playing!
Credo sia la nostra canzone!
KREH-do SEE-a la NOS-tra kan-ZO-neh!

Let's make a wish together.
Esprimiamo insieme un desiderio.
es-pree-mee-A-mo in-see-EH-meh oon deh-see-DEH-ree-o.

Is there anything that you want from me?
C'è qualcosa che vuoi da me?
cheh kwal-KO-sa keh voo-O-ee da MEH?

There is nowhere I would rather be than right here with you.
Non c'è altro luogo in cui vorrei essere se non qui con te.
*non cheh AL-tro loo-O-go in KOO-ee vor-REH-ee ES-seh-reh seh non KWEE
kon teh.*

I'll give you a ride back to your place.
Ti do un passaggio fino a casa.
tee do oon pas-SAJ-jee-o FEE-no a KA-sa.

Would you like me to hold your purse?
Vuoi che ti tenga la borsetta?
voo-O-ee keh tee TEN-ga la bor-SET-ta?

Let's pray before we eat our meal.
Preghiamo prima di mangiare.
preh-ghee-A-mo PREE-ma dee man-jee-A-reh.

Do you need a napkin?
Hai bisogno* di un tovagliolo*?
A-ee bee-SON-nee-o dee oon to-val-lee-O-loo?

I'm thirsty.
Ho sete.
o SEH-teh.

I hope you enjoy your meal.
Spero che tu ti goda il pasto.
SPEH-ro keh too tee GO-da eel POS-to.

I need to add more salt to the salt shaker.
Devo aggiungere del sale alla saliera.
DEH-vo aj-JOON-jeh-reh del SA-leh AL-la sa-lee-EH-ra.

We should get married!
Dovremmo sposarci!
do-VREM-mo spo-SAR-chee!

How old are you?
Quanti anni hai?
KWAN-tee AN-nee A-ee?

Will you dream of me?
Mi sognerai*?
mee son-nee-eh-RA-ee?

Thank you very much for the wonderful date last night.
Grazie davvero della meravigliosa* serata passata ieri.
*GRA-zee-eh dav-VER-ro DEL-la meh-ra-veel-lee-O-sa seh-RA-ta pas-SA-ta
ee-EH-ree.*

Would you like to come to a party this weekend?
Hai voglia* di andare ad una festa questo fine settimana?
*A-ee VOL-lee-a dee an-DA-reh ad OO-na FES-ta KWES-to FEE-ne set-tee-
MA-na?*

This Saturday night, right?
Questo sabato sera, vero?
KWES-to SA-ba-to SEH-ra, VEH-ro?

I will be lonely without you.
Mi sentirei solo senza di te.
mee sen-tee-REH-ee SO-lo SEN-za dee TEH.

Please stay the night?
Ti puoi fermare per la notte, per favore?*tee poo-O-ee fer-MA-reh per la
NOT-teh, per fa-VO-reh?*

I like your fragrance.
Mi piace il tuo profumo.
mee pee-A-cheh eel TOO-o pro-FOO-mo.

That is a beautiful outfit you're wearing.
Quello che indossi è un bellissimo completo.
KWEL-lo keh in-DOS-see EH oon bel-LEES-see-mo kom-PLEH-to.

You look beautiful.
Sei bellissima.
SEH-ee bel-LEES-see-ma.

Let me help you out of the car.
Lascia che ti aiuti ad uscire dall'automobile.
LA-shee-a keh tee a-ee-OO-tee ad oo-SHEE-reh DAL- la-oo-to-MO-bee-leh.

Sarah, will you come with me to dinner?
Sarah, vuoi venire a cena con me?
Sarah, voo-O-ee veh-NEE-reh a CHEH-na kon meh?

I would like to ask you out on a date.
Vorrei chiederti di uscire con me.
vor-REH-ee kee-EH-der-tee dee oo-SHEE-reh kon meh.

Are you free tonight?
Sei libera stasera?
SEH-ee LEE-beh-ra sta-SEH-ra?

This is my phone number. Call me anytime.
Questo è il mio numero di telefono. Chiamami quando vuoi.
KWES-to EH eel MEE-o NOO-meh-ro dee teh-LEH-fo-no. kee-A-ma-mee
KWAN-do voo-O-ee.

Can I hug you?
Posso abbracciarti?
POS-so ab-bra-chee-AR-tee?

Would you like to sing karaoke?
Vorresti cantare al karaoke?
vor-RES-tee kan-TA-reh al karaoke?

What kind of song would you like to sing?
Che tipo di canzone vorresti cantare?
keh TEE-po dee kan-ZO-neh vor-RES-tee kan-TA-reh?

Have you ever sung this song before?
Hai mai cantato questa canzone prima d'ora?
A-ee MA-ee kan-TA-to KWES-ta kan-ZO-neh PREE-ma DO-ra?

We can sing it together.
Possiamo cantarla assieme.
pos-see-A-mo kan-TAR-la in-see-EH-meh.

Can I kiss you?
Posso baciarti?
POS-so ba-chee-AR-tee?

Are you cold?
Hai freddo?
A-ee FRED-do?

We can stay out as late as you want.
Possiamo stare fuori quanto ti pare.
pos-see-A-mo STA-reh foo-O-ree KWAN-to tee PA-reh.

Please, dinner is on me.
Per favore, la cena la offro io.
per fa-VO-reh, la CHEH-na la OF-fro EE-o.

Shall we split the bill?
Ci dividiamo il conto?
CHEE dee-vee-dee-A-mo eel KON-to?

We should spend more time together.
Dovremmo trascorrere più tempo assieme.
do-VREM-mo tras-KOR-reh-reh PEW TEM-po as-see-EH-meh.

We should walk the town tonight.
Dovremmo camminare per la città questa sera.
do-VREM-mo kam-mee-NA-reh per la chit-TA KWES-ta SEH-ra.

Did you enjoy everything?
Ti è piaciuto tutto?
tee EH pee-a-chee-OO-to TOOT-to?

MONEY AND SHOPPING

May I try this on?
Posso provarlo?
POS-so pro-VAR-lo?

How much does this cost?
Quanto costa?
KWAN-to KOS-ta?

Do I sign here or here?
Firmo qui o qui?
FEER-mo KWEE o KWEE?

Is that your final price?
È questo il prezzo finale?
EH KWES-to eel PREZ-zo fee-NA-leh?

Where do I find toiletries?
Dove trovo i prodotti da bagno*?
DO-ve TRO-vo ee pro-DOT-tee da BAN-nee-o?

Would you be willing to take five dollars for this item?
Accetterebbe cinque dollari per questo oggetto?
a-chet-teh-REB-beh CHIN-kweh DOL-la ree per KWES-to oj-JET-to?

I can't afford it at that price.
Non posso permettermelo a quel prezzo.
non POS-so per-MET-ter-meh-lo a KWEL PREZ-zo.

I can find this cheaper somewhere else.
Posso trovarlo ad un prezzo migliore* da un'altra parte.
POS-so tro-VAR-lo ad oon PREZ-zo meel-lee-O-reh da oo-NAL-tra PAR-teh.

Is there a way we can haggle on price?
C'è un modo per trattare sul prezzo?
cheh oon MO-do per trat-TA-reh sool PREZ-zo?

107

How many of these have sold today?
Quanti di questi sono stati venduti oggi?
KWAN-tee dee KWES-tee SO-no STA-tee ven-DOO-tee OJ-jee?

Can you wrap that up as a gift?
Può fare una confezione regalo?
poo-O FA-re OO-na kon-feh-zee-O-neh reh-GA-lo?

Do you provide personalized letters?
Fornite anche messaggi personalizzati?
for-NEE-te AN-keh mes-SAJ-jee per-so-na-leez-ZA-tee?

I would like this to be special delivered to my hotel.
Vorrei che mi venisse consegnato* in albergo.
vor-REH-ee keh mee veh-NIS-seh kon-sen-nee-A-to in al-BER-go.

Can you help me, please?
Può aiutarmi, per favore?
poo-O a-ee-oo-TAR-mee, per fa-VO-reh?

We should go shopping at the market.
Dovremmo andare a fare la spesa al mercato.
do-VREM-mo an-DA-reh a FA-reh la SPEH-sa al mer-KA-to.

Are you keeping track of the clothes that fit me?
Stai annotando i vestiti che mi vanno bene?
STA-ee ann-O-TAN-do ee ves-TEE-tee keh mee VAN-no BEH-neh?

Can I have one size up?
Posso averlo di una taglia* più grande?
POS-so a-VER-lo dee OO-na TAL-lee-a PEW GRAN-deh?

How many bathrooms does the apartment have?
Quanti bagni* ha l'appartamento?
KWAN-tee BAN-nee a lap-par-ta-MEN-to?

Where's the kitchen?
Dov'è la cucina?
do-VEH la koo-CHEE-na?

Does this apartment have a gas or electric stove?
Quest'appartamento ha i fornelli a gas o elettrici?
kwest-ap-par-ta-MEN-to a ee for-NEL-lee a gas o eh-LET-tree-chee?

Is there a spacious backyard?
C'è un giardino spazioso?
cheh oon jee-ar-DEE-no spa-zee-O-so?

How much is the down payment?
Quant'è l'acconto?
kwant-EH lak-KON-to?

I'm looking for a furnished apartment.
Cerco un appartamento arredato.
CHER-ko oon ap-par-ta-MEN-to ar-reh-DA-to.

I need a two bedroom apartment to rent.
Ho bisogno* di un appartamento con due stanze da letto in affittare.
o bee-SO-nee-o dee oon ap-par-ta-MEN-to kon DOO-eh STAN-zeh da LET-to in af-fit-to.

I'm looking for an apartment with utilities paid.
Cerco un appartamento con le bollette comprese.
CHER-ko oon ap-par-ta-MEN-to kon leh bol-LET-teh kom-PREH-she.

The carpet in this apartment needs to be pulled up.
La moquette in questo appartamento dev'essere eliminata.
la mo-KETT in KWES-to ap-par-ta-MEN-to dev-ES-seh-reh eh-lee-mee-NA-ta.

I need you to come down on the price of this apartment.
Ho bisogno* che abbassi il prezzo di questo appartamento.
O bee-SON-nee-o keh ab-BAS-see eel PREZ-zo dee KWES-to ap-par-ta-MEN-to.

Will I be sharing this place with other people?
Condividerò questo posto con altre persone?
kon-dee-vee-deh-RO KWES-to POS-to kon AL-treh per-SO-neh?

How do you work the fireplace?
Come funziona il camino?
KO-meh foon-zee-O-na eel ka-MEE-no?

Are there any curfew rules attached to this apartment?
Ci sono delle regole sul coprifuoco per questo appartamento?
chee SO-no DEL-leh REH-go-leh SOOL ko-pree-foo-O-ko per KWES-to ap-par-ta-MEN-to?

How long is the lease for this place?
Quanto dura il contratto d'affitto di questo posto?
KWAN-to DOO-ra eel kon-TRAT-to daf-FEET-to dee KWES-to POS-to?

Do you gamble?
Giochi d'azzardo?
jee-O-kee daz-ZAR-do?

We should go to a casino.
Dovremmo andare al casinò.
do-VREM-mo an-DA-reh al ka-see-NO.

There is really good horse racing in this area.
C'è un ippodromo davvero buono in questa zona.
cheh oon ip-PO-dro-mo dav-VEH-ro boo-O-no in KWES-ta ZO-na.

Do you have your ID so that we can go gambling?
Hai con te la carta d'identità, così possiamo andare a giocare d'azzardo?
A-ee kon teh la KAR-ta dee-den-tee-TA, KO-see pos-see-A-mo an-DA-reh a jee-o-KA-reh daz-ZAR-do?

Who did you bet on?
Su chi hai scommesso?
soo kee A-ee skom-MES-so?

I am calling about the apartment that you placed in the ad.
Chiamo per l'appartamento che avete messo nell'annuncio.
kee-A-mo per lap-par-ta-MEN-to keh -A-veh-teh MESS-o nehl an-NOON-chee-o.

How much did you bet?
Quanto hai scommesso?
KWAN-to A-ee skom-MES-so?

We should go running with the bulls!
Dovremmo andare a correre con i tori!
do-VREM-mo an-DA-reh a KOR-reh-reh kon ee TO-ree!

Is Adele coming to sing at this venue tonight?
Adele verrà a cantare a questo indirizzo stasera?
Adele ver-RA a kan-TA-reh a KWES-to in-dee-REEZ-zo sta-SEH-ra?

How much is the item you have in the window?
Quanto costa l'oggetto in vetrina?
KWAN-to KOS-ta loj-JET-to in veh-TREE-na?

Do you have payment plans?
Offrite dei finanziamenti?
of-FREE-teh DEH-ee fee-nan-zee-a-MEN-tee?

Do these two items come together?
Questi due oggetti vengono venduti assieme?
KWES-tee DOO-eh oj-JET-tee VEN-go-no ven-DOO-tee as-see-EH-meh?

Are these parts cheaply made?
Queste parti sono di bassa qualità?
KWES-teh PAR-tee SO-no dee BAS-sa kwa-lee-TA?

This is a huge bargain!
Questo è un vero affare!
KWES-to EH oon VEH-ro af-FA-reh!

I like this. How does three hundred dollars sound?
Mi piace. Cosa ne pensa di trecento dollari?
mee pee-A-cheh. KO-sa neh PEN-sa dee treh-CHEN-to DOL-la-ree?

Two hundred is all I can offer. That is my final price.
Duecento è tutto quello che posso offrire. Questo è il mio ultimo prezzo.
doo-eh-CHEN-to EH TOOT-to KWEL-lo keh POS-so of-FREE-reh. KWES-to EH eel MEE-o OOL-tee-mo PREZ-zo.

Do you have cheaper versions of this item?
Ha una versione più economica di questo oggetto?
a OO-na er-see-O-neh PEW eh-ko-NO-mee-ka dee KWES-to oj-JET-to?

Do you have the same item with a different pattern?
Ha lo stesso oggetto in una fantasia differente?
a lo STES-so oj-JET-to in OO-na fan-ta-SEE-a dif-feh-REN-teh?

How much is this worth?
Quanto vale questo?
KWAN-to VA-leh KWES-to?

Can you pack this up and send it to my address on file?
Può impacchettarlo e spedirmelo a questo indirizzo?
poo-OH im-pak-ket-TAR-meh-lo eh speh-DEER-meh-lo a KWES-to in-dee-RIZ-zo?

Does it fit?
Te lo senti bene?
Teh lo SEN-teeBEH-neh?

They are too big for me.
Sono troppo grandi per me.
SO-no TROP-po GRAN-dee per meh.

Please find me another but in the same size.
Per favore, me ne trovi un altro, ma della stessa taglia*.
per fa-VO-reh, meh neh TRO-vee oon AL-tro, ma DEL-la STES-sa TAL-lee-a.

It fits, but is tight around my waist.
Va bene, ma è stretto attorno alla vita.
va BEH-neh, ma EH STRET-to AL-la VEE-ta.

Can I have one size down?
Posso averlo di una taglia* più piccola?
POS-so a-VER-lo dee OO-na TAL-lee-a PEW PEEK-ko-la?

Size twenty, American.
Taglia* venti americana.
TAL-lee-a VEN-tee a-meh-ree-KA-na.

Do you sell appliances for the home?
Vendete elettrodomestici per la casa?
ven-DEH-teh eh-let-tro-do-MES-tee-chee per la KA-sa?

Not now, thank you.
Non ora, grazie.
non O-ra, GRA-zee-eh.

I'm looking for something special.
Sto cercando qualcosa di speciale.
sto cher-KAN-do kwal-KO-sa dee speh-chee-A-leh.

I'll call you when I need you.
Ti chiamerò quando avrò bisogno* di te.
tee kee-a-meh-RO KWAN-do a-VRO bee-SON-nee-o dee teh.

Do you have this in my size?
Lo avete della mia taglia*?
lo a-VEH-teh DEL-la MEE-a TAL-lee-a?

On which floor can I find cologne?
A che piano posso trovare l'acqua di colonia?
a keh pee-A-no POS-so tro-VA-reh LAK-kwa dee ko-LON-nee-a?

Where is the entrance?
Dov'è l'entrata?
dov-EH len-TRA-ta?

Do I exit from that door?
Posso uscire da quella porta?
POS-so oo-SHEE-reh da KWEL-la POR-ta?

Where is the elevator?
Dov'è l'ascensore?
dov-EH la-SHEN-zo-reh?

Do I push or pull to get this door open?
Devo spingere o tirare per aprire la porta?
DEH-vo SPEEN-jeh-reh o tee-RA-reh per a-PREE-reh la POR-ta?

I already have that, thanks.
Ce l'ho già, grazie.
cheh-LO jee-A, GRA-zee-eh.

Where can I try this on?
Dove posso provarlo?
DO-ve POS-so pro-VAR-lo?

This mattress is very soft.
Il materasso è molto soffice.
EEL ma-teh-RAS-so EH MOL-to SOF-fee-cheh.

What is a good place for birthday gifts?
Qual è un bel posto per i regali di compleanno?
kwal-EH oon bel POS-to per ee reh-GA-lee dee kom-pleh-AN-no?

I'm just looking, but thank you.
Sto solo guardando, ma grazie.
sto SO-lo gwar-DAN-do, ma GRA-zee-eh.

Yes, I will call you when I need you, thank you.
Sì, la chiamerò quando avrò bisogno*, grazie.
see, la kee-a-meh-RO KWAN-do a-VRO bee-SON-nee-o, GRA-zee-eh.

Do you accept returns?
Accettate anche i resi?
a-chet-TA-teh AN-keh ee REH-see?

Here is my card and receipt for the return.
Ecco qui la mia carta e lo scontrino per il reso.
EK-ko KWEE la MEE-a KAR-ta eh lo skon-TREE-no per eel REH-so.

Where are the ladies clothes?
Dove sono i vestiti da donna?
DO-ve SO-no ee ves-TEE-tee da DON-na?

What sizes are available for this item?
Quali taglie* sono disponibili per quest'articolo?
KWA-lee TAL-lee-eh SO-no dis-po-NEE-bee-lee per kwes-tar-TEE-ko-lo?

Is there an ATM machine nearby?
C'è un bancomat nelle vicinanze?
CHEH oon BAN-ko-mat NEL-leh vee-chee-NAN-zeh?

What forms of payment do you accept?
Che metodi di pagamento accetate?
keh MEH-to-dee dee pa-ga-MEN-to a-CHET-ta-teh?

That doesn't interest me.
Questo non mi interessa.
KWES-to non meen-teh-RES-sa.

I don't like it, but thank you.
Non mi piace, ma grazie.
non mee pee-A-cheh, ma GRA-zee-eh.

Do you take American dollars?
Accettate anche dollari americani?
a-chet-TA-teh AN-keh DOL-la-ree a-meh-ree-KA-nee?

Can you make change for me?
Potrebbe cambiarmeli?
po-TREB-beh kam-bee-AR-meh-lee?

What is the closest place to get change for my money?
Qual è il posto più vicino dove poter cambiare i soldi?
kwal-EH eel POS-to PEW vee-CHEE-no DO-veh po-TER kam-bee-A-reh ee SOL-dee?

Are travelers checks able to be changed here?
Si possono cambiare i travel check qui?
see POS-so-no kam-bee-A-reh ee travel check KWEE?

What is the current exchange rate?
Qual è l'attuale tasso di cambio?
kwal-EH lat-too-A-leh TAS-so dee KAM-bee-o?

What is the closest place to exchange money?
Qual è il posto più vicino per cambiare valuta?
kwal-EH eel POS-to PEW vee-CHEE-no per kam-bee-A-reh la va-LOO-ta?

Do you need to borrow money? How much?
Hai bisogno* di farti prestare dei soldi? Quanti?
A-ee bee-SON-nee-o dee FAR-tee pres-TA-reh DEH-ee SOL-dee? KWAN-tee?

Can this bank exchange my money?
Si può cambiare valuta in questa banca?
see poo-O kam-bee-A-reh va-LOO-ta in KWES-ta BAN-ka?

What is the exchange rate for the American dollar?
Qual è il tasso di cambio per i dollari americani?
kwal-EH eel TAS-so di KAM-bee-o per ee DOL-la-ree a-meh-ree-KA-nee?

Will you please exchange me fifty dollars?
Mi cambieresti cinquanta dollari?
mee kam-bee-eh-RES-tee chin-KWAN-ta DOL-la-ree?

I would like a receipt with that.
Vorrei una ricevuta per quello.
vor-REH-ee OO-na ree-cheh-VOO-ta per KWEL-lo.

Your commission rate is too high.
Il vostro tasso di commissione è troppo alto.
eel VOS-tro TAS-so dee kom-mis-see-O-neh EH TROP-po AL-to.

Does this bank have a lower commission rate?
Questa banca ha un tasso di commissione più basso?
KWES-ta BAN-ka a oon TAS-so dee kom-mis-see-O-neh PEW BAS-so?

Do you take cash?
Accettate contanti?
a-chet-TA-teh kon-TAN-tee?

Where can I exchange dollars?
Dove posso cambiare dollari?
DO-veh POS-so kam-bee-A-reh DOL-la-ree?

I want to exchange dollars for yen.
Vorrei cambiare dollari con yen.
vor-REH-ee kam-bee-A-reh DOL-la-ree kon ee-EN.

116

Do you take credit cards?
Accettate carte di credito?
a-chet-TA-te KAR-te dee CREH-dee-to?

Here is my credit card.
Ecco la mia carta di credito.
EK-ko la MEE-a KAR-ta dee CREH-dee-to.

One moment, let me check the receipt.
Un attimo, lasciatemi controllare la ricevuta.
oon AT-tee-mo, la-shee-A-teh-mee kon-trol-LA-reh la ree-cheh-VOO-ta.

Do I need to pay tax?
Devo pagare le tasse?
DEH-vo pa-GA-reh leh TAS-seh?

How much is this item with tax?
Quanto costa questo oggetto con le tasse?
KWAN-to KOS-ta KWES-to oj-JET-to kon leh TAS-seh?

Where is the cashier?
Dov'è il cassiere?
do-VEH eel kas-see-EH-reh?

Excuse me, I'm looking for a dress.
Mi scusi, sto cercando un vestito.
mee SKOO-see, sto cher-KAN-do oon ves-TEE-to.

That's a lot for that dress.
È un prezzo alto per questo vestito.
EH oon PREZ-zo AL-to per KWES-to ves-TEE-to.

Sorry, but I don't want it.
Mi spiace ma non lo voglio*.
mee spee-A-cheh, ma non lo VOL-lee-o.

Okay I will take it.
Ok, lo prenderò.
Ok, lo pren-deh-RO.

I'm not interested if you are going to sell it at that price.
Non mi interessa se viene venduto a quel prezzo.
non min-teh-RES-sa seh vee-EH-neh ven-DOO-to a KWEL PREZ-zo.

You are cheating me at the current price.
Per questo prezzo sembra un imbroglio*.
per KWES-to PREZ-zo SEM-bra oon im-BROL-lee-o.

No thanks. I'll only take it if you lower the price by half.
No, grazie. Lo prenderò solamente se il prezzo sarà dimezzato.
no, GRA-zee-eh. lo pren-deh-RO so-la-MEN-teh seh eel PREZ-zo sa-RA dee-mez-ZA-to.

That is a good price, I'll take it.
Questo è un buon prezzo, lo prenderò.
KWES-to EH oon boo-ON PREZ-zo, lo pren-deh-RO.

Do you sell souvenirs for tourists?
Vendete souvenirs per turisti?
ven-DEH-teh souvenirs per too-RIS-tee?

Can I have a bag with that?
Potrei avere anche una borsa?
po-TREH-ee a-VEH-reh AN-keh OO-na BOR-sa?

Is this the best bookstore in the city?
Questa è la migliore* libreria in città?
KWES-ta EH la meel-lee-OR lee-breh-REE-a in chit-TA?

I would like to go to a game shop to buy comic books.
Vorrei andare in un negozio di giochi per comprare dei fumetti.
vor-REH-ee an-DA-reh in oon neh-GO-zee-o dee jee-O-kee per kom-PRA-reh DEH-ee foo-MET-tee.

Are you able to ship my products overseas?
È in grado di spedire il prodotto oltreoceano?
eh in GRA-do dee speh-DEE-reh il pro-DOT-to ol-treh-O-cheh-A-no?

CHILDREN AND PETS

Which classroom does my child attend?

Che classe frequenta mio figlio*?

keh KLAS-seh freh-koo-EN-ta MEE-o FEEL-lee-o?

Is the report due before the weekend?

La relazione è da consegnare* prima del fine settimana?

la reh-la-zee-O-neh EH da kon-seh-nee-A-reh PREE-ma del FEE-neh set-tee-MA-na?

I'm waiting for my mom to pick me up.

Sto aspettando che mia mamma mi venga a prendere.

sto as-pet-TAN-do keh MEE-a MAM-ma mee VEN-ga a PREN-deh-reh.

What time does the school bus run?

A che ora passa l'autobus della scuola?

a keh O-ra PAS-sa LA-oo-to-boos DEL-la skoo-O-la?

I need to see the principal.

Devo vedere il preside.

DEH-vo veh-DEH-reh eel PREH-see-deh.

I would like to report bullying.

Vorrei riportare un caso di bullismo.

vor-REH-ee ree-por-TA-reh oon KA-so dee bool-LEES-mo.

What are the leash laws in this area?

Quali sono le regole riguardo ai guinzagli* in questa zona?

KWA-lee SO-no leh REH-go-leh ree-GWAR-do A-ee goo-in-ZAL-lee in KWEs-ta ZO-na?

Please keep your dog away from mine.

Per favore, tenga il suo cane lontano da me.

per fa-VO-reh, TEN-ga eel SOO-o KA-neh lon-TA-no da meh.

My dog doesn't bite.
Il mio cane non morde.
eel MEE-o KA-neh non MOR-deh.

I am allergic to cat hair.
Sono allergico al pelo di gatto.
SO-no al-LER-jee-ko al PE-lo dee GAT-to.

Don't leave the door open or the cat will run out!
Non lasciare la porta aperta o il gatto scapperà!
non la-shee-A-reh la POR-ta a PER-ta o eel GAT-to skap-peh-RA!

Have you fed the dogs yet?
Hai già dato da mangiare ai cani?
A-ee JA DA-to da man-jee-A-reh A-ee KA-nee?

We need to take the dog to the veterinarian.
Dobbiamo portare il cane dal veterinario.
dob-bee-A-mo por-TA-reh eel KA-neh dal veh-teh-ree-NA-ree-o.

Are there any open roster spots on the team?
C'è un posto da titolare in squadra?
CHEH oon POS-to da tee-to-LA-reh in skoo-A-dra?

My dog is depressed.
Il mio cane è depresso.
eel MEE-o KA-neh EH deh-PRES-so.

Don't feed the dog table scraps.
Non dar da mangiare le briciole al cane.
non DAR da man-jee-A-reh leh BREE-chee-o-leh al KA-neh.

Don't let the cat climb up on the furniture.
Non lasciare che il gatto si arrimpichi sui mobili.
non la-shee-A-reh keh eel GAT-to see ar-RAM-pee-kee SOO-ee MO-bee-lee.

The dog is not allowed to sleep in the bed with you.
Il cane non può dormire a letto con te.
eel KA-neh non poo-O dor-MEE-reh a LET-to kon teh.

There is dog poop on the floor. Clean it up.
C'è cacca di cane sul pavimento. Puliscila.
CHEH KAK-ka dee KA-neh sool pa-vee-MEN-to. poo-LEE-shee-la.

When was the last time you took the dog for a walk?
Quand'è stata l'ultima volta che hai portato il cane a fare una passeggiata?
kwan-DEH STA-ta LOOL-tee-ma VOL-ta keh A-ee por-TA-to eel KA-neh a FA-reh OO-na pas-sej-jee-A-ta?

Are you an international student? How long are you attending?
Sei uno studente internazionale? Da quanto tempo frequenti questa scuola?
SEH-ee OO-no stoo-DEN-teh in-ter-na-zee-o-NA-leh? da KWAN-to TEM-po fre-KWEN-tee KWES-ta skoo-O-la?

Are you a French student?
Sei uno studente francese?
SEH-ee OO-no stoo-DEN-teh fran-CHEH-seh?

I am an American student that is here for the semester.
Sono uno studente americano che starà qui per un semestre.
SO-no OO-no stoo-DEN-teh a-meh-ree-KA-no keh sta-RA KWEE per oon seh-MES-treh.

Please memorize this information.
Per favore, memorizza queste informazioni.
per fa-VO-reh, meh-mo-REEZ-za KWES-teh in-for-ma-zee-O-nee.

This is my roommate Max.
Questo è il mio compagno* di stanza Max.
KWES-to EH eel MEE-o kom-PAN-nee-o dee STAN-za Max.

Are these questions likely to appear on the exams?
Queste domande saranno presenti nell'esame?
KWES-te do-MAN-deh sa-RAN-no preh-SEN-tee all-eh-SA-me?

Teacher, say that once more please.
Professore, lo dica di nuovo, per favore.
pro-fes-SO-reh, lo DEE-ka dee noo-O-vo, per fa-VO-reh.

I didn't do well on the quiz.
Il quiz non mi è andato tanto bene.
eel koo-EEZ non mee EH and-DA-to TAN-to BEH-neh eel koo-EEZ.

Go play outside, but stay where I can see you.
Vai a giocare fuori, ma stai dove io possa vederti.
VA-ee a jee-o-KA-reh foo-O-ree, ma STA-ee DO-ve EE-o POS-sa ve-DER-tee.

How is your daughter?
Come sta tua figlia*?
KO-meh STA TOO-a FEEL-lee-a?

I'm going to walk the dogs.
Vado a portare fuori i cani.
VA-do a por-TA-reh foo-O-ree ee KA-nee.

She's not very happy here.
Lei non è molto felice qui.
LEH-ee non EH MOL-to feh-LEE-cheh KWEE.

I passed the quiz with high marks!
Ho passato il test con voti alti!
o pas-SA-to eel test kon VO-tee AL-tee!

What program are you enrolled in?
A quale programma ti sei iscritto?
A KWA-leh pro-GRAM-ma tee SEH-ee is-KREET-to?

I really like my English teacher.
Mi piace davvero il mio insegnante* di inglese.
mee pee-A-cheh dav-VEH-ro eel MEE-o in-sen-nee-AN-teh din-GLEH-seh.

I have too much homework to do.
Ho troppi compiti da fare.
o TROP-pee KOM-pee-tee da FA-reh.

Tomorrow, I have to take my dog to the vet.
Domani devo portare il mio cane dal veterinario.
do-MA-nee DEH-vo por-TA-reh eel MEE-o KA-neh dal veh-teh-ree-NA-ree-o.

When do we get to go to lunch?
A che ora andiamo a pranzo?
a KEH O-ra an-dee-A-mo a PRAN-zo?

My dog swallowed something he shouldn't have.
Il mio cane ha ingoiato una cosa che non avrebbe dovuto.
eel MEE-o KA-neh a in-go-ee-A-to OO-na KO-sa keh non a-VREB-beh do-VOO-to.

We need more toys for our dog to play with.
Ci servono più giocattoli per il nostro cane.
chee SER-vo-no PEW jee-o-KAT-to-lee per eel NOS-tro KA-neh.

Can you please change the litter box?
Potresti, per favore, cambiare la lettiera?
po-TRES-tee, per fa-VO-reh, kam-bee-A-reh la let-tee-EH-ra?

Get a lint brush and roll it to get the hair off your clothes.
Prendi una spazzola e togliti* i peli dai vestiti.
PREN-dee OO-na SPAZ-zola e TOL-lee-tee ee PEH-lee DA-ee ves-TEE-tee.

Can you help me study?
Mi puoi aiutare con lo studio?
mee poo-O-ee a-ee-oo-TA-reh kon lo STOO-dee-o?

I have to go study in my room.
Devo andare a studiare nella mia camera.
DEH-vo an-DA-reh a stoo-dee-A-reh nehl-la mee-A ka-meh-ra.

We went to the campus party and it was a lot of fun.
Siamo andati alla festa del campus e ci siamo divertiti molto.
see-A-mo an-DA-tee AL-la FES-ta del KAM-poos e chee see-A-mo dee-ver-TEE-tee MOL-to.

Can you use that word in a sentence?
Puoi usare quella parola in una frase?
poo-O-ee oo-SA-reh KWEL-la pa-RO-la in OO-na FRA-seh?

How do you spell that word?
Puoi fare lo spelling di quella parola?
poo-O-ee FA-reh lo spelling dee KWEL-la pa-RO-la?

Go play with your brother.
Vai a giocare con tuo fratello.
VA-ee a jee-o-KA-reh kon TOO-o fra-TEL-lo.

Come inside! It is dinnertime.
Vieni dentro! È ora di cena.
vee-EH-nee DEN-tro! EH O-ra dee cheh-NA.

Tell me about your day.
Parlami della tua giornata.
PAR-la-mee DEL-la TOO-a jee-or-NA-ta.

Is there anywhere you want to go?
Ti va di andare da qualche parte?
tee va dee an-DA-reh da KWAL-keh PAR-teh?

How are you feeling?
Come ti senti?
KO-meh tee SEN-tee?

What do you want me to make for dinner tonight?
Cosa vorresti che ti cucinassi per cena stasera?
KO-sa vor-RES-tee keh tee koo-chee-NAS-see per CHEH-na sta-SEH-ra?

It's time for you to take a bath.
È giunta l'ora che ti faccia un bagno*.
EH jee-OON-ta LO-ra keh tee FA-chee-a oon BAN-nee-o.

Brush your teeth and wash behind your ears.
Lavati i denti e anche dietro le orecchie.
LA-va-tee ee DEN-tee e AN-keh dee-EH-tro leh o-REK-kee-eh.

You're not wearing that to bed.
Non metterti questa roba per andare a letto.
non MET-ter-tee KWES-ta RO-ba per an-DA-reh a LET-to.

I don't like the way you're dressed. Put something else on.
Non mi piace il modo in cui sei vestito. Mettiti qualcos'altro.
non mee pee-A-cheh eel MO-do in KOO-ee SEH-ee ves-TEE-to. MET-tee-tee kwal-kos-AL-tro.

Did you make any friends today?
Ti sei fatto degli* amici oggi?
tee SEH-ee FAT-to DEL-lee a-MEE-chee OJ-jee?

Let me see your homework.
Fammi vedere i tuoi compiti.
FAM-mee veh-DEH-reh ee too-O-ee KOM-pee-tee.

Do I need to call your school?
Devo chiamare la tua scuola?
DEH-vo kee-a-MA-reh la skoo-O-la?

The dog can't go outside right now.
Il cane non può uscire in questo momento.
eel KA-neh non poo-O oos-CHEE-re in KWES-to mo-MEN-to.

Is the new quiz going to be available next week?
Il nuovo quiz sarà disponibile la prossima settimana?
eel noo-O-vo KWEEZ sa-RA dis-po-NEE-bee-leh la PROS-see-ma set-tee-MA-na?

Are we allowed to use calculators with the test?
Possiamo utilizzare la calcolatrice durante il test?
pos-see-A-mo oo-tee-leez-ZA-re la kal-ko-la-TREE-cheh doo-RAN-teh eel test?

I would like to lead today's lesson.
Vorrei condurre io la lezione di oggi.
vor-REH-ee kon-DOOR-reh EE-o la leh-zee-O-neh dee OJ-jee.

I have a dorm curfew so need to go back.
Devo rispettare il coprifuoco e devo tornare.
DEH-vo ris-pet-TA-reh eel ko-pree-foo-O-ko eh DEH-vo tor-NA-reh.

Do I have to use pencil or ink?
Devo usare la matita o la penna?
DEH-vo oo-SA-reh la ma-TEE-ta o la PEN-na?

Are cell phones allowed in class?
I cellulari sono permessi in classe?
ee chel-loo-LA-ree SO-no per-MES-see in KLAS-seh?

125

Where can I find the nearest dog park?
Dove posso trovare il parco per cani più vicino?
DO-veh POS-so tro-VA-reh eel PAR-ko per KA-nee PEW vee-CHEE-no?

Are dogs allowed to be off their leash here?
I cani possono stare senza guinzaglio* qui?
ee KA-nee POS-so-no STA-reh SEN-za goo-in-ZAL-lee-o KWEE?

Are children allowed here?
I bambini sono ammessi qui?
ee bam-BEE-nee SO-no am-MES-see KWEE?

I would like to set up a play date with our children.
Vorrei organizzare un incontro per far giocare insieme i nostri bambini.
vor-REH-ee or-ga-niz-ZA-reh oon in-KON-tro per far jee-o-KA-reh in-see-EH-meh ee NOS-tree bam-BEE-nee.

I would like to invite you to my child's birthday party.
Vorrei invitarti al compleanno di mio figlio*.
vor-REH-ee in-vee-TAR-tee al kom-pleh-AN-no dee MEE-o FEEL-lee-o.

Did you miss your dorm curfew last night?
Non hai rispettato il coprifuoco ieri notte?
non A-ee ris-pet-TA-to eel ko-pree-foo-O-ko ee-EH-ree NOT-teh?

TRAVELER'S GUIDE

Over there is the library.
Laggiù c'è la biblioteca.
laj-jee-OO CHEH la bee-blee-o-TEH-ka.

Just over there.
Proprio laggiù.
PRO-pree-o laj-jee-OO.

Yes, this way.
Sì, di qua.
SEE, dee KWA.

I haven't done anything wrong.
Non ho fatto nulla di male.
non o FAT-to NOOL-la dee MA-leh.

It was a misunderstanding.
C'è stato un malinteso.
CHEH STA-to oon ma-leen-TEH-so.

I am an American citizen.
Sono un cittadino americano.
SO-no oon chit-ta-DEE-no a-meh-ree-KA-no.

We are tourists on vacation.
Siamo turisti in vacanza.
see-A-mo too-RIS-tee in va-KAN-za.

I am looking for an apartment.
Sto cercando un appartamento.
sto cher-KAN-do oon ap-par-ta-MEN-to.

This is a short-term stay.
Questo è un soggiorno breve.
KWES-to EH oon soj-jee-OR-no BREH-veh.

I am looking for a place to rent.
Sto cercando un posto da prendere in affitto.
sto cher-KAN-do oon POS-to da PREN-deh-reh in af-FEET-to.

Where can we grab a quick bite to eat?
Dove possiamo mangiare un boccone?
DO-veh pos-see-A-mo man-jee-A-reh oon bok-KO-neh?

We need the cheapest place you can find.
Ci serve il posto più economico che tu possa trovare.
chee SER-veh eel POS-to PEW e-ko-NO-mee-ko keh too POS-sa tro-VA-reh.

Do you have a map of the city?
Hai una cartina della città?
A-ee OO-na kar-TEE-na DEL-la chit-TA?

What places do tourists usually visit when they come here?
Quali posti visitano di solito i turisti quando vengono qui?
KWA-lee POS-tee VEE-see-ta-no dee SO-lee-to ee too-RIS-tee KWAN-do VEN-go-no KWEE?

Can you take our picture, please?
Ci può fare una foto, per favore?
chee poo-O FA-reh OO-na FO-to, per fa-VO-reh?

Do you take foreign credit cards?
Accettate carte di credito straniere?
a-chet-TA-teh KAR-teh dee KREH-dee-to stra-nee-EH-reh?

I would like to hire a bicycle to take us around the city.
Vorrei noleggiare una bicicletta per fare un giro della città.
vor-REH-ee no-lej-jee-A-reh OO-na bee-chee-KLET-ta per FA-reh oon JEE-ro DEL-la chit-TA.

Do you mind if I take pictures here?
Ti spiace se faccio foto qui?
tee spee-A-cheh seh FA-chee-o FO-to KWEE?

ANSWERS

Yes, to some extent.
Sì, in un certo modo.
SEE, in oon CHER-to MO-do.

I'm not sure.
Non sono sicuro.
non SO-no see-KOO-ro.

Yes, go head.
Sì, fai pure.
SEE, FA-ee POO-reh.

Yes, just like you.
Sì, come te.
SEE, KO-meh teh.

No, no problem at all.
No, nessun problema.
no, nes-SOON pro-BLEH-ma.

This is a little more expensive than the other item.
Questo è un po' più costoso dell'altro oggetto.
KWES-to EH oon PO PEW kos-TO-so dell-AL-tro oj-JET-to.

My city is small, but nice.
La mia città è piccola, ma graziosa.
la MEE-a chit-TA EH PIK-ko-la ma gra-zee-O-sa.

This city is quite big.
La città è piuttosto grande.
la chit-TA EH pee-oot-TO-sto GRAN-deh.

I'm from America.
Sono americano.
SO-no a-meh-ree-KA-no.

We'll wait for you.
Ti aspetteremo.
tee as-pet-teh-REH-mo.

I love going for walks.
Adoro passeggiare.
a-DO-ro pas-sej-jee-A-reh.

I'm a woman.
Sono una donna.
SO-no OO-na DON-na.

Good, I'm going to see it.
Bene, lo vedrò.
BEH-neh, lo veh-DRO.

So do I.
Anch'io.
an-KEE-o.

I'll think about it and call you tomorrow with an answer.
Ci penserò e ti chiamerò domani per la risposta.
chee pen-seh-RO eh tee kee-a-meh-RO do-MA-nee per la ris-POS-ta.

I'm a parent to two children.
Sono genitore di due bambini. *SO-no je-nee-to-reh dee DOO-eh bam-BEE-nee.*

Does this place have a patio?
Questo posto non ha un patio?
KWES-to POS-to non a oon patio?

No, the bathroom is vacant.
No, il bagno* è libero.
no, eel BAN-nee-o EH LEE-beh-ro.

I'm not old enough.
Non sono abbastanza grande.
non SO-no ab-bas-TAN-za GRAN-deh.

No, it is very easy.
No, è molto semplice.
no, EH MOL-to SEM-plee-cheh.

Understood.
Capito.
ka-PEE-to.

Only if you go first.
Solo se ci vai per primo.
SO-lo seh chee VA-ee per PREE-mo.

Yes, that is correct.
Sì, è corretto.
SEE, EH kor-RET-to.

That was the wrong answer.
Questa era la risposta sbagliata*.
KWES-ta EH-ra la ris-POS-ta sbal-lee-A-ta.

We haven't decided yet.
Non abbiamo ancora deciso.
non ab-bee-A-mo an-KO-ra de-CHEE-so.

We can try.
Possiamo provare.
pos-see-A-mo pro-VA-reh.

I like to read books.
Mi piace leggere libri.
mee pee-A-cheh LEJ-jeh-reh LEE-bree.

We can go there together.
Ci possiamo andare assieme.
chee pos-see-A-mo an-DA-reh as-see-EH-meh.

Yes, I see.
Sì, capisco.
SEE, ka-PEES-ko.

That looks interesting.
Sembra interessante.
SEM-bra in-teh-res-SAN-teh.

Me neither.
Nemmeno io.
nem-MEH-no EE-o.

It was fun.
È stato divertente.
EH STA-to dee-ver-TEN-teh.

Me too.
Anche io.
AN-keh ee-O.

Stay there.
Stai lì.
STA-ee LEE.

We were worried about you.
Eravamo preoccupati per te.
eh-ra-VA-mo preh-ok-koo-PA-tee per teh.

No, not really.
No, non esattemente.
no, non eh-sat-ta-MEN-teh.

Unbelievable.
Incredibile.
in-kreh-DEE-bee-leh.

No, I didn't make it in time.
No, non ho fatto in tempo.
no, non o FAT-to in TEM-po.

No, you cannot.
No, non puoi.
no, non poo-O-ee.

Here you go.
Eccoti qua.
EK-ko-tee KWA.

It was good.
Era buono.
EH-ra boo-O-no.

Ask my wife.
Chiedi a mia moglie*.
kee-EH-dee a MEE-a MOL-lee-eh.

That's up to him.
Tocca a lui.
TOK-ka a LOO-ee.

That is not allowed.
Questo non è permesso.
KWES-to non EH per-MES-so.

You can stay at my place.
Puoi stare da me.
poo-O-ee STA-reh da meh.

Only if you want to.
Solo se lo vuoi.
SO-lo seh lo voo-O-ee.

It depends on my schedule.
Dipende dai miei impegni*.
dee-PEN-deh DA-ee mee-EH-ee im-PEN-nee.

I don't think that's possible.
Non credo sia possibile.
non KREH-do SEE-a pos-SEE-bee-leh.

You're not bothering me.
Non mi stai disturbando.
non mee STA-ee dis-toor-BAN-do.

The salesman will know.
Il venditore lo saprà.
eel ven-dee-TO-reh lo sa-PRA.

I have to work.
Devo lavorare.
DEH-vo la-vo-RA-reh.

I'm late.
Sono in ritardo.
SO-no in ree-TAR-do.

To pray.
Per pregare.
per preh-GA-reh.

I'll do my best.
Farò del mio meglio*.
fa-RO del MEE-o MEL-lee-o.

DIRECTIONS

Over here.
Laggiù.
laj-JOO.

Go straight ahead.
Vai sempre dritto.
VA-ee SEM-preh DRIT-to.

Follow the straight line.
Segui la linea dritta.
SEH-goo-ee la LEE-neh-a DRIT-ta.

Go halfway around the circle.
Vai fino a metà della rotonda.
VA-ee FEE-no a meh-TA DEL-la ro-TON-da.

It is to the left.
Si trova a destra.
see TRO-va a DES-tra.

Where is the party going to be?
Dove avrà luogo la festa?
DO-veh a-VRA loo-O-go la FES-ta?

Where is the library situated?
Dove si trova la biblioteca?
DO-veh see TRO-va la bee-blee-o-TEH-ka?

It is to the North.
Si trova a nord.
see TRO-va a nord.

You can find it down the street.
Lo troverai lungo la strada.
lo tro-veh-RA-ee LOON-go la STRA-da.

135

Go into the city to get there.
Entra in città per arrivare lì.
EN-tra in chit-TA per ar-ree-VA-reh LEE.

Where are you now?
Dove sei adesso?
DO-veh SEH-ee a-DES-so?

There is a fire hydrant right in front of me.
C'è un idrante proprio davanti a me.
CHEH oon-ee-DRAN-teh PRO-pree-o da-VAN-tee a meh.

Do you know a shortcut?
Conosci una scorciatoia?
ko-NO-shee OO-na skor-chee-a-TO-ee-a?

Where is the freeway?
Dov'è la tangenziale?
dov-EH la tan-jen-zee-A-leh?

Do I need exact change for the toll?
Mi servono i soldi giusti per il pedaggio?
mee SER-von-o ee SOL-dee jee-OOS-tee per eel peh-DAJ-jee-o?

At the traffic light turn right.
Al semaforo gira a destra.
al seh-MA-fo-ro JEE-ra a DES-tra.

When you get to the intersection turn left.
Quando arrivi all'incrocio, gira a sinistra.
KWAN-do ar-ree-VEE all-in-KRO-chee-o JEE-ra a see-NIS-tra.

Stay in your lane until it splits off to the right.
Stai nella tua corsia fino a che non si divide a destra.
STA-ee NEL-la TOO-a kor-SEE-a FEE-no a KEH non see dee-VEE-de a DES-tra.

Don't go onto the ramp.
Non andare sulla rampa.
non an-DA-reh SOOL-al RAM-pa.

You are going in the wrong direction.
Stai andando nella direzione sbagliata*.
STA-ee an-DAN-do NEL-la dee-reh-zee-O-neh sbal-lee-A-ta.

Can you guide me to this location?
Puoi guidarmi verso questo luogo?
poo-O-ee gwee-DAR-mee VER-so KWES-to loo-O-go?

Stop at the crossroads.
Fermati all'incrocio.
FER-ma-tee all-in-KRO-chee-o.

You missed our turn. Please turn around.
Hai mancato l'uscita. Per favore, torna indietro.
A-ee man-KA-to loo-SHEE-ta. per fa-VO-reh, TOR-na in-dee-EH-tro.

It is illegal to turn here.
È illegale girare qui.
EH il-leh-GA-leh jee-RA-reh KWEE.

We're lost, could you help us?
Ci siamo persi, ci può aiutare?
chee see-A-mo PER-see, chee poo-OH a-ee-oo-TA-reh?

APOLOGIES

Dad, I'm sorry.
Papà, mi spiace.
pa-PA, mee spee-A-cheh.

I apologize for being late.
Mi scuso per il ritardo.
mee SKOO-so per eel ree-TAR-do.

Excuse me for not bringing money.
Mi scuso per non aver portato i soldi.
mee SKOO-so per non a-VER por-TA-to ee SOL-dee.

That was my fault.
È stata colpa mia.
EH STA-ta KOL-pa MEE-a.

It won't happen again, I'm sorry.
Non succederà di nuovo, mi spiace.
non soo-che-deh-RA dee noo-O-vo, mee- spee-A-cheh.

I won't break another promise.
Non infrangerò un'altra promessa.
non in-fran-jeh-RO oon-AL-tra pro-MES-sa.

You have my word that I'll be careful.
Hai la mia parola che starò attento.
A-ee la MEE-a pa-RO-la keh sta-RO at-TEN-to.

I'm sorry, I wasn't paying attention.
Mi spiace, non stavo ascoltando.
mee spee-A-cheh, non STA-vo as-kol-TAN-do.

I regret that. I'm so sorry.
Me ne pento. Mi dispiace tanto. *meh neh PEN-to. mee dis-pee-A-chehTAN-to.* **I'm sorry, but today I can't.**
Mi spiace, ma oggi non posso.
mee spee-A-cheh, ma OJ-jee non POS-so.

It's not your fault, I'm sorry.
Non è colpa tua, mi spiace.
non EH KOL-pa TOO-a, mee spee-A-cheh.

Please, give me another chance.
Per favore, dammi un'altra possibilità.
per fa-VO-reh, DAM-mee oo-NAL-tra pos-see-bee-lee-TA.

Will you ever forgive me?
Mi perdonerai mai?
mee per-do-neh-RA-ee MA-ee?

I hope in time we can still be friends.
Spero che col tempo potremo essere ancora amici. *SPEH-ro keh kol TEM-po po-TREH-mo ES-seh-reh an-KO-ra a-MEE-chee.*

I screwed up, and I'm sorry.
Ho fatto un casino e mi dispiace.
o FAT-to oon ka-SEE-no eh mee dis-pee-A-cheh.

SMALL TALK

No.	Yes.	Okay.	Please.
No.	Sì.	Okay.	Per favore.
no.	*see.*	*okay.*	*per fa-VO-reh.*

Do you fly out of the country often?
Voli spesso fuori dal paese?
VO-lee SPES-so foo-O-ree dal pa-EH-seh?

Thank you.
Grazie.
GRA-zee-eh.

That's okay.
Va bene così.
va BEH-neh ko-SEE.

I went shopping.
Sono andato a fare shopping.
SO-no an-DA-to a FA-reh shopping.

There.
Lì.
lee.

Very well.
Molto bene.
MOL-to BEH-neh.

What?
Cosa?
KO-sa?

I think you'll like it.
Credo ti piacerà.
KREH-do tee pee-a-cheh-RA.

When.
Quando.
KWAN-do.

I didn't sleep well.
Non ho dormito bene.
non o dor-MEE-to BEH-neh.

Until what time?
Fino a che ora?
FEE-no a keh O-ra?

We are waiting in line.
Stiamo aspettando in fila.
stee-A-mo as-pet-TAN-do in FEE-la.

We're only waiting for a little bit longer.
Aspetteremo solo un altro po'.
as-pet-teh-REH-mo SO-lo oon AL-tro PO.

How.
Come.
KO-meh.

Where?
Dove?
DO-veh?

I'm glad.
Sono contento.
SO-no kon-TEN-to.

You are very tall.
Sei molto alto.
SEH-ee MOL-to AL-to.

I like to speak your language.
Mi piace parlare la tua lingua.
mee pee-A-cheh par-LA-reh la TOO-a LIN-goo-a.

You are very kind.
Sei molto gentile.
SEH-ee MOL-to jen-TEE-leh.

Happy birthday!
Buon compleanno!
boo-ON kom-pleh-AN-no!

I would like to thank you very much.
Ti ringrazio davvero tanto.
tee rin-GRA-zee-o dav-VEH-ro TAN-to.

Here is a gift that I bought for you.
Qui c'è un regalo che ho preso per te.
KWEE cheh oon reh-GA-lo keh o PREH-so per teh.

Yes. Thank you for all of your help.
Sì. Grazie per il tuo aiuto.
see, GRA-zee-eh per TOOT-to eel TOO-o a-ee-OO-to.

What did you get?
Cos'hai preso?
KOS-a-ee PREH-so?

Have a good trip!
Fai buon viaggio!
FA-ee boo-ON vee-AJ-jee-o!

This place is very special to me.
Questo posto è molto speciale per me.
KWES-to POS-to EH MOL-to speh-chee-A-leh per meh.

My foot is asleep.
Mi si è addormentato un piede.
mee see EH ad-dor-men-TA-to oon pee-EH-deh.

May I open this now or later?
Devo aprirlo ora o più tardi?
DEH-vo a-PREER-lo O-ra o PEW TAR-dee?

Why do you think that is?
Perché pensi che sia così?
per-KEH PEN-see keh SEE-a ko-SEE?

Which do you like better, chocolate or caramel?
Quale ti piace di più, cioccolato o caramello?
KWA-leh tee pee-A-cheh dee PEW, chok-ko-LA-to o ka-ra-MEL-lo?

Be safe on your journey.
Fai attenzione quando sei in viaggio.
FA-ee at-ten-zee-O-neh KWAN-do SEH-ee in vee-AJ-jee-o.

I want to do this for a little longer.
Vorrei farlo ancora per un po'.
vor-REH-ee FAR-lo an-KO-ra per oon PO.

This is a picture that I took at the hotel.
Questa è una foto che ho fatto in hotel.
KWES-ta eh OO-na FO-to keh o FAT-to in hotel.

Allow me.
Permettimi.
per-MET-tee-mee.

I was surprised.
Ero sorpreso.
EH-ro sor-PREH-so.

I like that.
Mi piace.
mee pee-A-cheh.

Are you in high spirits today?
Sei su di giri oggi?
SEH-ee soo dee JEE-ree OJ-jee?

Oh, here comes my wife.
Oh, arriva mia moglie*.
o, ar-REE-va MEE-a MOL-lee-eh.

Can I see the photograph?
Posso vedere la fotografia?
POS-so veh-DEH-reh la fo-to-gra-FEE-a?

Feel free to ask me anything.
Sentiti libero di chiedermi tutto.
SEN-tee-tee LEE-beh-ro dee kee-EH-der-mee TOOT-to.

That was magnificent!
È stato magnifico*!
EH STA-to man-NEE-fee-ko!

See you some other time.
Ci vediamo un'altra volta.
CHEE veh-dee-A-mo oon-AL-tra VOL-ta.

No more, please.
Basta così, grazie.
BAS-ta ko-SEE, GRA-zee-eh.

Please don't use that.
Per favore, non lo usare.
per fa-VO-reh, non lo oo-SA-reh.

That is very pretty.
Questo è molto carino.
KWES-to eh MOL-to ka-REE-no.

Would you say that again?
Lo puoi dire di nuovo?
lo poo-O-ee DEE-reh dee noo-O-vo?

Speak slowly.
Parla lentamente.
PAR-la len-ta-MEN-teh.

I'm home.
Sono a casa.
SO-no a KA-sa.

Is this your home?
Questa è casa tua?
KWES-ta EH KA-sa TOO-a?

I know a lot about the area.
So un sacco di cose riguardo a questa zona.
so oon SAK-ko dee KO-se ree-GWAR-do a KWES-ta ZO-na.

Welcome back. How was your day?
Bentornato, com'è andata oggi?
ben-tor-NA-to, kom-EH an-DA-ta OJ-jee?

I read every day.
Leggo ogni* giorno.
LEG-go ON-nee jee-OR-no.

My favorite type of book are novels by Stephen King.
I miei libri preferiti sono i romanzi di Stephen King.
ee mee-EH-ee LEE-bree preh-feh-REE-tee SO-no ee ro-MAN-zee dee Stephen King.

You surprised me!
Mi hai sorpreso!
mee A-ee sor-PREH-so!

I am short on time so I have to go.
Ho poco tempo e devo andare.
o PO-ko TEM-po eh DEH-vo an-DA-reh.

Thank you for having this conversation.
Grazie per questa conversazione.
GRA-zee-eh per KWES-ta kon-ver-sa-zee-O-neh.

Oh, when is it?
Oh, quand'è?
o, kwand-EH?

This is my brother Jeremy.
Questo è mio fratello Jeremy.
KWES-to EH MEE-o fra-TEL-lo Jeremy.

That is my favorite bookstore.
Questo è il mio negozio di libri preferito.
KWES-to EH eel MEE-o neh-GO-zee-o dee LEE-bree pre-feh-REE-to.

That statue is bigger than it looks.
Quella statua è più grande di quel che sembra.
KWEL-la STA-too-a EH PEW GRAN-deh dee KWEL keh SEM-bra.

Look at the shape of that cloud!
Guarda la forma di quella nuvola!
GWAR-da la FOR-ma dee KWEL-la NOO-vo-la!

BUSINESS

I am president of the credit union.
Sono il presidente della cooperativa di credito.
SO-no eel preh-see-DEN-teh DEL-la ko-peh-ra-TEE-va dee KREH-dee-to.

We are expanding in your area.
Ci stiamo espandendo nella vostra zona.
CHEE stee-A-mo es-pan-DEN-do NEL-la VOS-tra ZO-na.

I am looking for work in the agriculture field.
Sto cercando lavoro nel campo agricolo.
sto cher-KAN-do la-VO-ro nel KAM-po a-GREE-ko-lo.

Sign here, please.
Firmi qui, per favore.
FEER-mee KWEE, per fa-VO-reh.

I am looking for temporary work.
Sto cercando un lavoro temporaneo.
sto cher-KAN-do oon la-VO-ro tem-po-RA-neh-o.

I need to call and set up that meeting.
Devo chiamare e organizzare quella riunione.
DEH-vo kee-a-MA-reh eh or-ga-neez-ZA-reh KWEL-la ree-oo-nee-O-neh.

Is the line open?
La linea è aperta?
la LEE-neh-a EH a-PER-ta?

I need you to hang up the phone.
Ho bisogno che riagganci il telefono.
o bee-SON-nee-o keh ree-A-GUN-cheeeel teh-LEH-fo-no.

Who should I ask for more information about your business?
A chi devo chiedere per ottenere più informazioni riguardo alla sua
azienda?
*a kee DEH-vo kee-EH-deh-reh per ot-teh-NEH-reh PEW in-for-ma-zee-O-
nee ree-goo-AR-do AL-la SOO-a a-zee-EN-da?*

There was no answer when you handed me the phone.
Non ha risposto nessuno quando mi hai passato il telefono.
*non a ris-POS-to nes-SOO-no KWAN-do mee A-ee pas-SA-to eel teh-LEH-fo-
no.*

Robert is not here at the moment.
Robert non è qui al momento.
Robert non EH KWEE al mo-MEN-to.

Call me after work, thanks.
Chiamami dopo il lavoro, grazie.
kee-A-ma-mee DO-po eel la-VO-ro, GRA-zee-eh.

We're strongly considering your contract offer.
Stiamo seriamente considerando la sua offerta di lavoro.
*stee-A-mo seh-ree-a-MEN-teh kon-see-deh-RAN-do la SOO-a of-FER-ta dee
la-VO-ro.*

Have the necessary forms been signed yet?
Sono stati già firmati tutti i moduli necessari?
SO-no jee-A STA-tee fir-MA-tee TOOT-tee ee MO-doo-lee ne-ches-SA-ree?

I have a few hours available after work.
Ho alcune ore a disposizione dopo il lavoro.
o al-KOO-neh O-reh a dis-po-see-zee-O-neh DO-po eel la-VO-ro.

What do they make there?
Cosa fanno là?
KO-sa FAN-no la?

I have no tasks assigned to me.
Non ci sono compiti assegnati* a me.
Non chee SO-no KOM-pee-tee as-sen-nee-A-tee a meh.

How many workers are they hiring?
Quanti lavoratori assumeranno?
KWAN-tee la-vo-ra-TO-ree as-soo-meh-RAN-no?

It should take me three hours to complete this task.
Ci dovrebbero volere tre ore per completare il compito.
chee do-VREB-beh-ro vo-LEH-reh treh O-reh per kom-pleh-TA-reh eel KOM-pee-to.

Don't use that computer, it is only for financial work.
Non usare quel computer, si usa solo in ambito finanziario.
non oo-SA-reh KWEL computer, see OO-sa SO-lo in AM-bee-to fee-nan-zee-A-ree-o.

I only employ people that I can rely on.
Assumo solo persone sulle quali posso contare.
as-SOO-mo SO-lo per-SO-neh SOOL-leh KWA-lee POS-so kon-TA-reh.

After I talk to my lawyers we can discuss this further.
Dopo aver parlato con il mio avvocato ne potremo discutere.
DO-po a-VER-par-LA-to kon eel MEE-o av-vo-KA-to neh po-TREH-mo dis-KOO-teh-reh.

Are there any open positions in my field?
Ci sono posizioni disponibili nel mio campo?
chee SO-no po-see-zee-O-nee dis-po-nee-bee-lee nel MEE-o KAM-po?

I'll meet you in the conference room.
Ci vediamo nella sala conferenze.
chee veh-dee-A-mo NEL-la SA-la kon-feh-REN-zeh.

Call and leave a message on my office phone.
Chiama e lascia un messaggio al mio numero d'ufficio.
kee-A-ma eh LA-SHEE-a oon mes-SAJ-jee-o al MEE-o NOO-meh-ro doof-FEE-chee-o.

Send me a fax with that information.
Mandami un fax con quell'informazione.
MAN-da-mee oon fax con KWEL-lin-for-ma-zee-O-neh.

Hi, I would like to leave a message for Sheila.
Salve, vorrei lasciare un messaggio per Sheila.
SAL-veh, vor-REH-ee la-shee-A-reh oon mes-SAJ-jee-o per Sheila.

Please repeat your last name.
Per favore, ripeta il suo cognome*.
per fa-VO-reh, ree-PEH-ta eel SOO-o kon-nee-O-meh.

I would like to buy wholesale.
Vorrei comprare all'ingrosso.
vor-REH-ee kom-PRA-reh al-lin-GROS-so.

How do you spell your last name?
Può fare lo spelling del suo cognome*?
poo-O FA-reh lo spelling del SOO-o kon-nee-O-meh?

I called your boss yesterday and left a message.
Ho chiamato il suo capo ieri e ho lasciato un messaggio.
o kee-a-MA-to eel SOO-o KA-po ee-EH-ree eh o la-shee-A-to oon mes-SAJ-jee-o.

That customer hung up on me.
Quel cliente mi ha agganciato il telefono.
kwel klee-EN-teh mee a ag-gan-chee-A-to eel teh-LEH-fo-no.

She called but didn't leave a callback number.
Lei ha chiamato ma non ha lasciato un numero per poterla richiamare.
LEH-ee a kee-a-MA-to ma non a la-shee-A-to oon NOO-meh-ro per po-TER-la ree-kee-a-MA-reh.

Hello! Am I speaking to Bob?
Salve! Parlo con Bob?
SAL-veh! PAR-lo kon Bob?

Excuse me, but could you speak up? I can't hear you.
Mi scusi, potrebbe parlare più forte? Non la sento.
mee SKOO-see, po-TREB-beh par-LA-reh PEW FOR-teh? non la SEN-to.

The line is very bad, could you move to a different area so I can hear you better?
La linea è disturbata, potrebbe andare in un'altra zona così da poterla sentire meglio*?
la LEE-neh-a EH dis-toor-BA-ta, po-TREB-beh an-DA-reh in oon-AL-tra ZO-na ko-SEE da po-TER-la sen-TEE-reh MELlee-o?

I would like to apply for a work visa.
Vorrei candidarmi per un permesso di lavoro.
vor-REH-ee kan-dee-DAR-mee per oon per-MES-so dee la-VO-ro.

It is my dream to work here teaching the language.
Il mio sogno* è lavorare qui insegnando* la mia lingua.
eel MEE-o SON-ne-o EH la-vo-RA-reh KWEE in-sen-nee-AN-do la MEE-a LIN-goo-a.

I have always wanted to work here.
Ho sempre voluto lavorare qui.
O SEM-preh vo-LOO-to la-vo-RA-reh KWEE.

Where do you work?
Dove lavori?
DO-veh la-VO-ree?

Are we in the same field of work?
Lavoriamo nello stesso ambito?
la-vo-ree-A-mo NEL-lo STES-so AM-bee-to?

Do we share an office?
Condividiamo un ufficio?
kon-dee-vee-dee-A-mo oon oof-FEE-chee-o?

What do you do for a living?
Cosa fai per vivere?
KO-sa FA-ee per VEE-veh-reh?

I work in the city as an engineer for Cosco.
Lavoro in città come ingegnere* per Cosco.
la-VO-ro in chit-TA KO-meh in-jen-nee-EH-reh per Cosco.

I am an elementary teacher.
Sono un maestro elementare.
SO-no oon ma-ES-tro eh-leh-men-TA-reh.

What time should I be at the meeting?
A che ora devo essere alla riunione?
a keh O-ra DEH-vo ES-seh-reh AL-la ree-oo-nee-O-neh?

Would you like me to catch you up on what the meeting was about?
Vuoi che ti metta a conoscenza riguardo all'argomento dell'incontro?
voo-O-ee keh tee MET-ta a ko-no-SHEN-za ree-GWAR-do all-ar-go-MEN-to del-lin-KON-tro?

I would like to set up a meeting with your company.
Vorrei organizzare un incontro con la vostra azienda.
vor-REH-ee or-ga-niz-ZA-reh oon in-KON-tro kon la VOS-tra a-zee-EN-da.

Please, call my secretary for that information.
Per favore, chiami la mia segretaria per quell'informazione.
per fa-VO-reh, kee-A-mee la MEE-a seh-greh-TA-ree-a per kwell-in-for-ma-zee-O-neh.

I will have to ask my lawyer.
Dovrò chiedere al mio avvocato.
do-VRO kee-EH-deh-reh-al MEE-o av-vo-KA-to.

Fax it over to my office number.
Manda un fax al numero del mio ufficio.
MAN-da oon fax al NOO-meh-ro dell-oof-FEE-chee-o.

Will I have any trouble calling into the office?
Avrò dei problemi a chiamare in ufficio?
a-VRO DEH-ee pro-BLEH-mee a kee-a-MA-reh in oof-FEE-chee-o?

Do you have a business card I can have?
Avrebbe un biglietto* da visita da darmi?
a-VREB-beh oon beel-lee-ET-to da VEE-see-ta da DAR-mee?

Here is my business card. Please, take it.
Ecco il mio biglietto* da visita. Per favore, lo prenda.
EK-ko eel MEE-o oon beel-lee-ET-to da VEE-see-ta. per fa-VO-reh, lo PREN-da.

My colleague and I are going to lunch.
Il mio collega e io andremo a pranzo.
ee mee-O kol-LEH-ga e EE-o an-DREH-mo a PRAN-zo.

I am the director of finance for my company.
Sono il direttore finanziario della mia azienda.
SO-no eel dee-ret-TO-reh fee-nan-zee-A-ree-o DEL-la MEE-a a-zee-EN-da.

I manage the import goods of my company.
Mi occupo di importare beni per la mia azienda.
mee OK-koo-po dee im-por-TA-reh BEH-nee per la MEE-a a-zee-EN-da.

My colleagues' boss is Steven.
Il capo dei miei colleghi è Steven.
eel KA-po DEH-ee mee-EH-ee kol-LEH-ghee EH Steven.

I work for the gas station company.
Lavoro per l'azienda del gas.
la-VO-ro per la-zee-EN-da del gas.

What company do you work for?
Per quale azienda lavori?
per KWA-leh a-zee-EN-da la-VO-ree?

I'm an independent contractor.
Sono un imprenditore indipendente.
SO-no oon im-pren-dee-TO-reh in-dee-pen-DEN-teh.

How many employees do you have at your company?
Quanti impiegati ha presso la sua azienda?
KWAN-tee im-pee-eh-GA-tee a PRES-so la SOO-a a-zee-EN-da?

I know a lot about engineering.
So un sacco di cose riguardo all'ingegneria*.
so oon SAK-ko dee KO-seh ree-goo-AR-do all-in-jen-nee-eh-REE-a.

I can definitely resolve that dispute for you.
Posso risolvere la questione per te.
POS-so ree-SOL-veh-reh-la kwes-tee-O-neh per teh.

You should hire an interpreter.
Dovresti assumere un interprete.
do-VRES-tee as-SOO-meh-reh oon in-TER-preh-teh.

Are you hiring any additional workers?
Assumerai altri lavoratori?
as-soo-meh-RA-ee AL-tree la-vo-ra-TO-ree?

How much experience do I need to work here?
Quanta esperienza mi serve per lavorare qui?
KWAN-ta es-peh-ree-EN-za mee SER-veh per la-vo-RA-reh KWEE?

Our marketing manager handles that.
Se ne occuperà il nostro responsabile del marketing.
seh neh ok-koo-peh-RA eel NOS-tro res-pon-SA-bee-leh del marketing.

I would like to poach one of your workers.
Vorrei assumere uno dei tuoi lavoratori.
vor-REH-ee as-SOO-meh-reh OO-no DEH-ee too-O-ee la-vo-ra-TO-ree.

Can we work out a deal that is beneficial for the both of us?
Possiamo pensare ad un accordo che porti benefici a tutti e due?
pos-see-A-mo pen-SA-reh ad oon ak-KOR-do keh POR-tee beh-neh-FEE-chee a TOOT-tee eh DOO-eh?

My resources are at your disposal.
Le mie risorse sono a vostra disposizione.
leh MEE-eh ree-SOR-seh SO-no a VOS-tra dis-po-see-zee-O-neh.

I am afraid that we have to let you go.
Temo che dovremo lasciarla andare.
TEH-mo keh do-VREH-mo la-shee-AR-la an-DA-reh.

This is your first warning. Please don't do that again.
Questo è il primo avvertimento. Per favore, non lo fare più.
KWES-to EH eel PREE-mo av-ver-tee-MEN-to. per fa-VO-reh, non lo FA-reh PEW.

File a complaint with HR about the incident.
Invia un reclamo alle Risorse Umane riguardo l'accaduto.
in-VEE-a oon reh-KLA-mo AL-leh ree-SOR-seh oo-MA-neh ree-goo-AR-do l-ak-ka-DOO-to.

Who is showing up for our lunch meeting?
Chi verrà al nostro incontro per pranzo?
kee ver-RA al NOS-tro in-KON-tro per PRAN-zo?

Clear out the rest of my day.
Liberami il resto della giornata.
LEE-beh-ra-mee eel RES-to DEL-la jee-or-NA-ta.

We need to deposit this into the bank.
Dobbiamo depositarlo in banca.
dob-bee-A-mo deh-po-see-TAR-lo in BAN-ka.

Can you cover the next hour for me?
Puoi coprirmi per la prossima ora?
poo-O-ee ko-PREER-mee per la PROS-see-ma O-ra?

If Shania calls, please push her directly through.
Se chiama Shania, passamela direttamente, grazie.
seh kee-A-ma Shania, PAS-sa-meh-la di-ret-ta-MEN-teh, GRA-zee-eh.

I'm leaving early today.
Me ne vado prima oggi.
meh neh VA-do PREE-ma OJ-jee.

I'll be working late tonight.
Lavorerò fino a tardi stanotte.
la-vo-reh-RO FEE-no a TAR-dee stah-NOT-teh.

You can use the bathroom in my office.
Puoi usare il bagno* nel mio ufficio.
poo-O-ee oo-SA-reh eel BAN-nee-o nel MEE-o oof-FEE-chee-o.

You can use my office phone to call out.
Puoi usare il telefono del mio ufficio per chiamare.
poo-O-ee oo-SA-reh eel teh-LEH-fo-no del MEE-o oof-FEE-chee-o per kee-a-MA-reh.

155

Please, close the door behind you.
Per favore, chiudi la porta dietro di te.
per fa-VO-reh, kee-OO-dee la POR-ta dee-EH-tro dee teh.

I need to talk to you privately.
Ho bisogno* di parlarti privatamente.
o bee-SON-nee-o dee par-LAR-tee pree-va-ta-MEN-te.

Your team is doing good work on this project.
il tuo team sta lavorando bene a questo progetto.
eel TOO-o team sta la-vo-RAN-do BE-ne a KWES-to pro-JET-to.

Our numbers are down this quarter.
Il nostro bilancio è in negativo questo trimestre.
eel NOS-tro bee-LAN-chee-o EH neh-ga-TEE-vo KWES-to tree-MES-treh.

I need you to work harder than usual.
Ho bisogno* che lavori più duramente del solito.
o bee-SON-nee-o keh la-VO-ree PEW doo-ra-MEN-teh del SO-lee-to.

I'm calling in sick today. Can anyone cover my shift?
Sono malato oggi. Qualcuno mi può sostituire?
SO-no ma-LA-to OJ-jee. kwal-KOO-no mee poo-O sos-tee-too-EE-reh?

Tom, we are thinking of promoting you.
Tom, stiamo pensando di darti una promozione.
Tom, stee-A-mo pen-SAN-do dee DAR-tee OO-na pro-mo-zee-O-neh.

I would like a raise.
Mi piacerebbe un aumento.
mee pee-a-cheh-REB-beh oon a-oo-MEN-to.

THE WEATHER

I think the weather is changing.
Credo che il tempo cambierà.
KREH-do keh eel TEM-po kam-bee-eh-RA.

Be careful, it is raining outside.
Stai attento, fuori sta piovendo.
STA-ee at-TEN-to, foo-O-ree sta pee-o-VEN-do.

Make sure to bring your umbrella.
Assicurati di portare l'ombrello.
as-see-KOO-ra-tee dee por-TA-reh lom-BREL-lo.

Get out of the rain or you will catch a cold.
Riparati dalla pioggia o ti prenderai un raffreddore.
ree-PA-ra-tee DAL-la pee-OJ-jee-a, o tee pren-deh-RA-ee oon raf-fred-DO-reh.

Is it snowing?
Sta nevicando?
sta neh-vee-KAN-do?

The snow is very thick right now.
La neve cade fitta in questo momento.
la NEH-veh KA-deh FIT-ta in KWES-to mo-MEN-to.

Be careful, the road is full of ice.
Stai attento, le strade sono piene di ghiaccio.
STA-ee at-TEN-to, leh STRA-deh SO-no pee-EH-neh dee ghee-A-chee-o.

What is the climate like here? Is it warm or cold?
Com'è il tempo qui? Caldo o freddo?
kom-EH eel TEM-po KWEE? KAL-do o FRED-do?

It has been a very nice temperature here.
C'è stata una temperatura davvero molto gradevole qui.
cheh STA-ta OO-na tem-peh-ra-TOO-ra dav-VEH-ro MOL-to GRA-deh-vo-leh KWEE.

Does it rain a lot here?
Piove parecchio qui?
pee-O-veh pa-REK-kee-o KWEE?

The temperature is going to break records this week.
Le temperature infrangeranno ogni* record questa settimana.
leh tem-peh-ra-TOO-reh in-fran-jeh-RAN-no ON-nee record KWES-ta set-tee-MA-na.

Does it ever snow here?
Nevica mai qui?
NEH-vee-ka MA-ee KWEE?

When does it get sunny?
Quando arriverà il sole?
KWAN-do ar-ree-veh-RA eel SO-le?

What's the forecast look like for tomorrow?
Cosa dicono le previsioni del tempo per domani?
KO-sa DEE-ko-no leh preh-vee-see-O-nee del TEM-po per do-MA-nee?

This is a heatwave.
Questa è un'ondata di caldo.
KWES-ta EH oon-on-DA-ta dee KAL-do.

Right now it is overcast, but should clear up by this evening.
Ora è nuvoloso, ma dovrebbe schiarirsi entro questa sera.
O-ra EH noo-vo-LO-so, ma do-VREB-beh skee-a-REER-see EN-tro KWES-ta SEH-ra.

It is going to heat up in the afternoon.
Si scalderà questo pomeriggio.
see skal-deh-RA KWES-to po-meh-REEJ-jee-o.

What channel is the weather channel?
Su che canale è il meteo?
soo keh ka-NA-leh EH eel MEH-teh-o?

Tonight it will be below freezing.
Questa notte ghiaccerà.
KWES-ta NOT-te ghee-a-cheh-RA.

It's very windy outside.
È davvero ventoso fuori.
EH dav-VEH-ro ven-TO-so foo-O-ree.

It's going to be cold in the morning.
Sarà freddo al mattino.
sa-RA FRED-do al mat-TEE-no.

It's not raining, only drizzling.
Non sta piovendo, solo piovigginando.
non sta pee-o-VEN-do, SO-lo pee-o-veej-jee-NAN-do.

HOTEL

I would like to book a room.
Vorrei prenotare una camera.
vor-REH-ee preh-no-TA-reh OO-na KA-meh-ra.

I'd like a single room.
Vorrei una stanza singola.
vor-REH-ee OO-na STAN-za SIN-go-la.

I'd like a suite.
Vorrei una suite.
vor-REH-ee OO-na suite.

How much is the room per night?
Quanto costa una stanza per notte?
KWAN-to KOS-ta OO-na STAN-za per NOT-teh?

How much is the room with tax?
Quanto costa la stanza tasse incluse?
KWAN-to KOS-ta la STAN-za TAS-seh in-KLOO-seh?

When is the checkout time?
A che ora si effettua il checkout?
a keh O-ra see ef-FET-too-a eel checkout?

I'd like a room with a nice view.
Vorrei una stanza con una bella vista.
vor-REH-ee OO-na STAN-za kon OO-na BEL-la VIS-ta.

I'd like to order room service.
Vorrei ordinare il servizio in camera.
vor-REH-ee or-dee-NA-reh eel ser-VEE-zee-o in KA-meh-ra.

Let's go swim in the outdoor pool.
Andiamo a nuotare nella piscina esterna.
an-dee-A-mo a noo-o-TA-reh NEL-la pee-SHEE-na.

Are pets allowed at the hotel?
Gli* animali sono ammessi in questo hotel?
lee a-nee-MA-lee SO-no am-MES-see in KWES-to hotel?

I would like a room on the first floor.
Vorrei una stanza al primo piano.
vor-REH-ee OO-na STAN-za al PREE-mo pee-A-no.

Can you send maintenance up to our room for a repair?
Può mandare la manutenzione in camera nostra per una riparazione?
poo-O man-DAR-eh la ma-noo-ten-zee-O-neh in KA-me-ra NOS-tra per OO-na ree-pa-ra-zee-O-neh?

I'm locked out of my room, could you unlock it?
Sono rimasto chiuso fuori dalla stanza, me la potrebbe aprire?
SO-no ree-MAS-to kee-OO-so foo-O-ree DAL-la STAN-za, meh la po-TREB-beh a-PREE-reh?

Our door is jammed and won't open.
La porta della nostra stanza si è bloccata e non si apre.
la POR-ta DEL-la NOS-tra STAN-za see EH blok-KA-ta eh non see A-preh.

How do you work the shower?
Come funziona la doccia?
KO-meh foon-zee-O-na la DO-chee-a?

Are the consumables in the room free?
I cibi e le bevande in camera sono gratis?
ee CHEE-bee-eh leh beh-VAN-deh in KA-meh-ra SO-no GRA-tees?

What is my final bill for the stay, including incidentals?
Quant'è la mia fattura finale, comprese le spese accessorie?
kwant-EH la MEE-a fat-TOO-ra fee-NA-leh, kom-PREH-seh leh SPEH-seh a-ches-SO-ree-eh?

Can you show me to my room?
Può mostrarmi dov'è la mia camera?
poo-O mos-TRAR-mee dov-EH la MEE-a KA-meh-ra?

Where can I get ice for my room?
Dove posso trovare del ghiaccio per la mia camera?
DO-ve POS-so tro-VA-reh del ghee-A-chee-o per la MEE-a KA-meh-ra?

Do you have any rooms available?
Avete delle camere disponibili?
a-VEH-teh DEL-leh ka-meh-reh dis-po-NEE-bee-lee?

Do you sell bottled water?
Vendete dell'acqua in bottiglia*?
ven-DEH-teh dell-AK-kwa in bot-TEEL-lee-a?

Our towels are dirty.
I nostri asciugamani sono sporchi.
ee NOS-tree a-shee-oo-ga-MA-nee SO-no SPOR-kee.

Have you stayed at this hotel before?
Siete mai stati in questo hotel prima?
see-EH-teh MA-ee STA-tee in KWES-to hotel PREE-ma?

How much is a room for two adults?
Quanto costa una camera per due adulti?
KWAN-to KOS-ta OO-na KA-meh-ra per DOO-eh a-DOOL-tee?

Does the room come with a microwave?
C'è un microonde in camera?
cheh oon mee-kro-ON-deh in KA-meh-ra?

May I see the room first? That way I will know if I like it.
Posso vedere la camera prima? In questo modo saprò se mi piace.
POS-so veh-DEH-reh la KA-meh-ra PREE-ma? In KWES-to mo-do SAP-ro seh mee PEE-a-che.

Do you have a room that is quieter?
Avete una stanza più tranquilla?
a-VEH-teh OO-na STAN-za PEW tran-KWIL-la?

How much is the deposit for my stay?
Quanto costa la cauzione per il mio soggiorno?
KWAN-to KOS-ta la ka-oo-zee-O-neh per il MEE-o soj-jee-OR-no?

Is the tap water drinkable at the hotel?
L'acqua di rubinetto è potabile in hotel?
LAK-kwa dee roo-bee-NET-to EH po-TA-bee leh in hotel?

Will there be any holds on my credit card?
Ci saranno delle trattenute sulla mia carta di credito?
chee sa-RAN-no del-leh trat-teh-noo-teh SOOL-la MEE-a KAR-ta dee KREH-dee-to?

Can I get a replacement room key?
Posso avere un'altra chiave per la mia stanza?
POS-so a-VEH-reh oo-NAL-tra kee-A-veh per la MEE-a STAN-za?

How much is a replacement room key?
Quanto costa una chiave di scorta?
KWAN-to KOS-ta OO-na kee-A-veh dee SKOR-ta?

Does the bathroom have a shower or a bathtub?
Il bagno* ha la doccia o la vasca?
eel BAN-nee-o a la DO-chee-a o la VAS-ka?

Are any of the channels on the tv available in English?
Ci sono canali tv disponibili in lingua inglese?
chee SO-no ka-NA-lee tee-VOO dis-po-NEE-bee-lee in LIN-gwa in-GLEH-seh?

I want a bigger room.
Vorrei una stanza più grande.
vor-REH-ee OO-na STAN-za PEW GRAN-deh.

Do you serve breakfast in the morning?
Servite la colazione al mattino?
ser-VEE-teh la ko-la-zee-O-neh al mat-TEE-no?

Oh, it's spacious.
Oh, è spaziosa.
o, EH spa-zee-O-sa.

My room is this way.
La mia stanza è di qua.
la MEE-a STAN-za EH dee KWA.

Straight down the hall.
Dritto in fondo al corridoio.
DRIT-to in FON-do al kor-ree-DO-ee-o.

Can you suggest a different hotel?
Può consigliarmi* un altro hotel?
poo-O kon-seel-lee-AR-mee oon-AL-tro hotel?

Does the room have a safe for my valuables?
La stanza ha una cassaforte per i miei oggetti di valore?
la STAN-za a OO-na kas-sa-FOR-teh per ee mee-EH-ee oj-JET-tee dee va-lo-REH ?

Please clean my room.
Per favore, pulisca la mia stanza.
per fa-vor-REH, mee poo-LIS-ka la MEE-a STAN-za.

Don't disturb me, please.
Non mi disturbi, per favore.
non mee dis-TOOR-bee, per fa-VO-reh.

Can you wake me up at noon?
Può svegliarmi* a mezzogiorno?
poo-O svel-lee-AR-me a mez-zo-jee-OR-no?

I would like to check out of my hotel room.
Vorrei effettuare il check out dalla mia camera d'albergo.
vor-REH-ee ef-fet-too-A-reh eel check out DAL-la MEE-a KA-meh-radal-BER-go.

Please increase the cleanup duty of my hotel room.
Per favore, migliorate* un po' le pulizie della mia camera d'albergo.
per fa-VO-reh, meel-lee-o-RA-teh oon PO leh poo-lee-ZEE-eh DEL-la MEE-a KA-meh-ra dal-BER-go.

Is the Marriott any good?
Il Marriott è buono?
eel Marriott EH boo-O-no?

Is it expensive to stay at the Marriott?
Costa tanto soggiornare al Marriott?
KOS-ta TAN-to soj-jee-or-NA-reh al Marriott?

I think our room has bedbugs.
Penso che nella nostra stanza ci siano delle cimici.
PEN-so keh NEL-la NOS-tra STAN-za chee SEE-a-no DEL-leh CHEE-mee-chee.

Can you send an exterminator to our room?
Può mandarmi un disinfestatore?
poo-O man-DAR-mee oon dee-sin-fes-ta-TO-reh?

I need to speak to your manager.
Devo parlare con il suo manager.
DE-vo par-LA-reh kon eel SOO-o manager.

Do you have the number to corporate?
Ha il numero della società aziendale?
a eel NOO-meh-ro DEL-la so-chee-eh-TA a-zee-en-DA-leh?

Does the hotel shuttle go to the casino?
La navetta dell'hotel va al casinò?
la na-VET-ta dell-o-TEL va al ka-see-NO?

Can you call me when the hotel shuttle is on its way?
Può chiamarmi quando la navetta dell'hotel sta per arrivare?
poo-O kee-a-MAR-mee KWAN-do la na-VET-ta dell-o-TEL sta per ar-ree-VA-reh?

Can we reserve this space for a party?
Possiamo prenotare questo spazio per una festa?
pos-see-A-mo pre-no-TA-reh KWES-to SPA-zee-o per OO-na FES-ta?

What is the guest limit for reserving an area?
Per quanti ospiti al massimo si può prenotare uno spazio??*per KWAN-tee OS-pee-tee al MAS-see-mo see poo-O pre-no-TA-reh OO-no SPA-zee-o ?*

What are the rules for reserving an area?
Quali sono le regole di prenotazione di uno spazio?
KWA-lee SO-no leh REH-go-leh dee preh-no-ta-zee-O-neh dee OO-no SPA-zee-o?

Can we serve or drink alcohol during our get together?

Possiamo servire o bere alcool durante l'incontro?

pos-see-A-mo ser-VEE-reh o BEH-reh AL-kol doo-RAN-teh lin-KON-tro?

I would like to complain about a noisy room next to us.

Mi vorrei lamentare per la stanza rumorosa a fianco della nostra.

mee vor-reh-ee la-men-TA-reh per la STAN-za roo-mo-RO-sa a fee-AN-ko DEL-la NOS-tra.

We have some personal items missing from our room.

Ci sono degli* oggetti personali che mancano dalla nostra stanza.

chee SO-no DEL-lee oj-JET-tee per-so-NA-lee keh MAN-ka-no DAL-la NOS-tra STAN-za.

SPORTS AND EXERCISE

Can we walk faster?
Possiamo camminare più velocemente?
pos-see-A-mo kam-mee-NA-reh PEW ve-lo-cheh-MEN-teh?

Do you want to go to a drag racetrack?
Vuoi andare su una pista da drag race?
voo-O-ee an-DA-reh soo OO-na PEE-sta da drag race?

Are you taking a walk?
Stai facendo una passeggiata?
STA-ee fa-CHEN-do OO-na pas-sej-jee-A-ta?

Do you want to jog for a kilometer or two?
Ti va di fare jogging per un chilometro o due?
tee va dee FA-reh jogging per oon kee-LO-meh-tro o DOO-eh?

How about fast walking?
Che ne dici di camminare velocemente?
keh neh DEE-chee dee kam-mee-NA-reh ve-lo-cheh-MEN-teh?

Would you like to walk with me?
Ti andrebbe di camminare con me?
tee an-DREB-beh dee kam-mee-NA-reh kon meh?

He is a really good player.
Lui è un giocatore molto bravo.
LOO-ee EH oon jee-o-ka-TO-reh MOL-to BRA-vo.

I feel bad that they traded him to the other team.
Mi spiace che l'abbia acquistato l'altra squadra.
mee spee-A-cheh keh LAB-bee-a ak-kwees-TA-to LAL-tra SKWA-dra.

Did you see that homerun?
Hai visto quel fuoricampo?
A-ee VIS-to KWEL foo-o-ree-KAM-po?

I have been a fan of that team for many years.
Sono stato un fan di quella squadra per molti anni.
SO-no STA-to oon fan dee KWEL-la SKWA-dra per MOL-tee AN-nee.

Who is your favorite team?
Qual è la tua squadra preferita?
kwal-EH la TOO-a SKWA-dra preh-feh-REE-ta?

Pele is my favorite player.
Pele è il mio giocatore preferito.
pe-LEH EH eel MEE-o jee-o-ka-TO-reh pre-feh-REE-to.

Do you like soccer?
Ti piace il calcio?
tee pee-A-cheh eel KAL-chee-o?

Do you watch American football?
Guardi il football americano?
GWAR-dee eel football a-meh-ree-KA-no?

Are there any games on right now?
Ci sono delle partite ora?
chee SO-no DEL-leh par-TEE-teh O-ra?

That was a bad call by the ref.
È stata una pessima chiamata arbitrale.
EH sta-TA OO-na PES-see-ma KIA-ma-ta AR-bee-tra-leh.

I put a lot of money on this game.
Ho scommesso un sacco di soldi su questa partita.
o skom-MES-so oon SAK-ko dee SOL-dee soo KWES-ta par-TEE-ta.

His stats have been incredible this season.
Le sue statistiche sono incredibili questa stagione.
leh SOO-eh sta-TIS-tee-keh SO-no in-kreh-DEE-bee-lee KWES-ta sta-jee-O-neh.

Do you want to play baseball today?
Vuoi giocare a baseball oggi?
voo-O-ee jee-o-KA-reh a baseball OJ-jee?

Let's go to the soccer field and practice.
Andiamo al campo da calcio ad allenarci.
an-dee-A-mo al KAM-po da KAL-chee-o ad al-leh-NAR-chee.

I am barely working up a sweat.
Sto a malapena sudando.
sto a ma-la-PEN-asoo-DAN-do.

Let's go to the gym and lift weights.
Andiamo in palestra a sollevare pesi.
an-dee-A-mo in pa-LES-tra a sol-leh-VA-reh PEH-see.

Give me more weights.
Dammi altri pesi.
DAM-mee AL-tree PEH-see.

Take some weights off.
Togli* un po' di pesi.
TOL-lee oon PO dee PEH-see.

Will you spot me?
Puoi controllarmi?
poo-O-ee kon-trol-LAR-mee?

How long do you want to run on the treadmill?
Per quanto vuoi correre sul tapis roulant?
per KWAN-to voo-O-ee KOR-reh-reh sool ta-PEE-roo-LAN?

Is this the best gym in the area?
È questala miglior* palestra in zona?
EH KWES-ta la meel-lee-OR pa-LES-tra in ZO-na?

Do I need a membership to enter this gym?
Ho bisogno* di una tessera per entrare in palestra?
o bee-SON-nee-o dee OO-na TES-seh-ra per en-TRA-reh in pa-LES-tra?

Do you have trial memberships for tourists?
Ci sono periodi di prova per turisti?
chee SO-no peh-REE-o-dee dee PRO-va per too-RIS-tee?

My muscles are still sore from the last workout.
I miei muscoli sono ancora doloranti dall'ultimo allenamento.
ee mee-EH-ee MOOS-ko-lee SO-no an-KO-ra do-lo-RAN-tee dall-OOL-tee-mo al-leh-na-MEN-to.

Give me a second while I adjust this.
Dammi un secondo mentre lo sistemo.
DAM-mee oon seh-KON-do MEN-treh lo sis-TEH-mo.

Time to hit the steam room!
È ora di andare a fare un bagno* turco!
EH O-ra dee an-DA-reh a FA-reh oon BA-nee-o TOOR-ko!

You can put that in my locker.
Puoi metterlo nel mio armadietto.
poo-O-ee MET-ter-lo nel MEE-o ar-ma-dee-ET-to.

I think we have to take turns on this machine.
Credo che dovremmo fare a turno su questa macchina.
KREH-do keh do-VREM-mo FA-reh a TOOR-no soo KWES-ta MAK-kee-na.

Make sure to wipe down the equipment when you are done.
Assicurati di pulire gli* attrezzi quando hai finito.
as-see-KOO-ra-tee dee poo-LEE-reh lee at-TREZ-zee KWAN-do A-ee fee-NEE-to.

Is there a time limit on working out here?
C'è un limite di tempo per allenarsi qui?
CHEH oon LEE-mee-teh dee TEM-po per al-leh-NAR-see KWEE?

We should enter a marathon.
Dovremmo partecipare a una maratona.
do-VREM-mo PAR-teh-chee-PAR-eh aOO-na ma-ra-TO-na.

How has your diet been going?
Come sta andando la tua dieta?
KO-meh STA an-DAN-do la TOO-a dee-EH-ta?

Are you doing keto?
Stai facendo keto?
STA-ee fa-CHEN-do KEH-to?

Make sure to stay hydrated while you work out.
Assicurati di idratarti mentre ti alleni.
as-see-KOO-ra-tee dee ee-dra-TAR-tee MEN-treh tee al-LEH-nee.

I'll go grab you a protein shake.
Ti vado a prendere un frullato proteico.
tee VA-do a PREN-deh-reh-oon frool-LA-to pro-TEH-ee-ko.

Do you want anything else? I'm buying.
Vuoi qualcos'altro? Offro io.
voo-O-ee kwal-kos-AL-tro? OF-fro EE-o.

I need to buy some equipment before I play that.
Devo comprarmi dell'attrezzatura prima di giocare.
DEH-vo kom-PRAR-mee del-lat-trez-za-TOO-ra PREE-ma dee jee-o-KAR-EH.

Do you want to spar?
Ti va di fare sparring?
tee va dee FA-reh sparring?

Full contact sparring.
Sparring di full contact.
sparring dee full contact.

Just a simple practice round.
Facciamo un semplice round di pratica.
fa-chee-A-mo oon SEM-plee-cheh round dee PRA-tee-ka.

Do you want to wrestle?
Vuoi fare wrestling?
voo-O-ee FA-reh wrestling?

What are the rules to play this game?
Quali sono le regole di questo gioco?
KWA-lee SO-no le REH-go-leh dee KWES-to jee-O-ko?

Do we need a referee?
Abbiamo bisogno* di un arbitro?
ab-bee-A-mo bee-SON-nee-o dee oon AR-bee-tro?

I don't agree with that call.
Non sono d'accordo con questa decisione.
non SO-no dak-KOR-do kon KWES-ta deh-chee-see-O-neh.

Can we get another opinion on that score?
Possiamo avere un'altra opinione su quella rete?
pos-see-A-mo a-VEH-reh oon-AL-tra o-pee-nee-O-neh soo KWEL-la REH-teh?

How about a game of table tennis?
Che ne dici di una partita di tennis da tavolo?
keh neh DEE-chee dee OO-na par-tee-ta dee tennis da TA-vo-lo?

Do you want to team up?
Vuoi fare squadra con me?
voo-O-ee FA-reh SKWA-dra kon meh?

Goal!
Goal!
Goal!

Homerun!
Fuoricampo!
foo-o-ree-KAM-po!

Touchdown!
Touchdown!
Touchdown!

Score!
Segna*!
sen-nee-A!

On your mark, get set, go!
Pronti, partenza, via!
PRON-tee, par-TEN-za, VEE-a!

Do you want to borrow my equipment?
Vuoi che ti presti la mia attrezzatura?
voo-O-ee keh tee PRES-tee la MEE-a at-trez-za-TOO-ra?

Hold the game for a second.
Ferma il gioco per un attimo.
FER-ma eel jee-O-ko per oon AT-tee-mo.

I don't understand the rules of this game.
Non capisco le regole di questo gioco.
non ka-PEES-ko leh REH-go-leh dee KWES-to jee-O-ko.

Timeout!
Timeout!
Timeout!

Can we switch sides?
Possiamo cambiare lato?
pos-see-A-mo kam-bee-A-reh LA-to?

There is something wrong with my equipment.
C'è qualcosa che non va con la mia attrezzatura.
cheh kwal-KO-sa keh non VA kon la MEE-a at-rez-za-TOO-ra.

How about another game?
Che ne dici di un'altra partita?
keh neh DEE-chee dee oon-AL-tra par-TEE-ta?

I would like a do over of that last game.
Vorrei rifare l'ultima partita.
vor-REH-ee ree-FA-reh LOOL-tee-MA par-TEE-ta.

Do want to go golfing?
Ti va di andare a giocare a golf?
tee va dee an-DA-reh a jee-o-KA-reh a golf?

Where can we get a golf cart?
Dove possiamo ottenere un golf cart?
DO-veh pos-see-A-mo ot-teh-NEH-reh oon golf kart?

Do you have your own clubs?
Avete i vostri stessi club?
a-VEH-teh ee VOS-tree STES-see club?

Would you like to play with my spare clubs?
Ti va di giocare con la mia seconda squadra?
tee va dee jee-o-KA-reh kon la MEE-a se-KON-da SKWA-dra?

How many holes do you want to play?
A quante buche vuoi giocare?
A KWAN-teh BOO-kehvoo-O-ee jee-o-KA-reh?

Do I have to be a member of this club to play?
Devo essere un membro di questo club per giocare?
DEH-vo ES-seh-reh oon MEM-bro dee KWES-to club per jee-o-KA-reh?

Let me ice this down, it is sore.
Fammici mettere del ghiaccio, mi fa male.
FAM-mee-chee MET-teh-reh del ghee-A-chee-o, mee fa MA-leh.

I can't keep up with you, slow down.
Non ce la faccio, rallenta.
non cheh la FA-chee-o, ral-LEN-ta.

Let's pick up the pace a little bit.
Aumentiamo un po' il ritmo.
a-oo-men-tee-A-mo oon PO eel RIT-mo.

Do you need me to help you with that?
Hai bisogno* che ti aiuti con questo?
A-ee bee-SON-nee-o keh tee a-ee-OO-tee kon KWES-to?

Am I being unfair?
Sono ingiusto?
SO-no in-jee-OOS-to?

Let's switch teams for the next game.
Cambiamo squadra per la prossima partita.
kam-bee-A-mo SKWA-dra per la PROS-see-ma par-TEE-ta.

Hand me those weights.
Passami quei pesi.
PAS-sa-mee KWEH-ee PEH-see.

THE FIRST 24 HOURS AFTER ARRIVING

When did you arrive?
Quando sei arrivato?
KWAN-do SEH-ee ar-ree-VA-to?

That was a very pleasant flight.
È stato un volo molto piacevole.
EH STA-to oon VO-lo MOL-to pee-a-CHEH-vo-leh.

Yes, it was a very peaceful trip. Nothing bad happened.
Sì, è stato un viaggio tranquillo. Non è successo niente di male.
SEE, EH STA-to oon vee-AJ-jee-o tran-KWIL-lo. non EH soo-CHES-so nee-EN-teh dee MA-leh.

I have jetlag so need to lay down for a bit.
Ho un po' di jetlag e ho bisogno* di stendermi un attimo.
o oon PO dee jetlag eh o bee-SON-nee-o dee STEN-der-mee oon AT-tee-mo.

No, that was my first time flying.
No, è stata la prima volta che ho volato.
no, EH STA-ta la PREE-ma VOL-ta keh o vo-LA-to.

When is the check in time?
A che ora è il check in?
a keh O-ra EH eel check in?

Do we need to get cash?
Abbiamo bisogno* di contante?
ab-bee-A-mo bee-SON-nee-o dee kon-TAN-teh?

How much money do you have on you?
Quanti soldi hai con te?
KWAN-tee SOL-dee A-ee kon teh?

How long do you want to stay here?
Per quanto tempo vuoi stare qui?
per KWAN-to TEM-po voo-O-ee STA-reh KWEE?

Do we have all of our luggage?
Abbiamo tutti i nostri bagagli*?
ab-bee-A-mo TOOT-tee ee NOS-tree ba-GAL-lee?

Let's walk around the city a bit before checking in.
Facciamo in giro in città prima di fare il check in.
fa-chee-A-mo oon JEE-ro in CHIT-ta PREE-ma dee FA-reh eel check in.

When is check in time for our hotel?
A che ora è il check in per il nostro hotel?
a keh O-ra EH il check in per eel NOS-tro hotel?

I'll call the landlord and let him know we landed.
Chiamo il padrone di casa e gli* dico che siamo atterrati.
kee-A-mo eel pa-DRO-neh dee KA-sa eh lee DEE-ko keh see-A-mo at-ter-RA-tee.

Let's find a place to rent a car.
Troviamo un posto dove noleggiare un'automobile.
tro-vee-A-mo oon POS-to DO-veh no-lej-jee-A-reh OO- na-oo-to-MO-bee-leh.

Let's walk around the hotel room and make sure it's correct.
Facciamo un giro nella camera dell'hotel per assicurarci che sia giusta.
fa-chee-A-mo oon JEE-ro NEL-la KA-meh-ra del-lo-TEL per as-see-koo-RAR-chee keh SEE-a jee-OOS-ta.

We'll look at our apartment and make sure everything is in order.
Diamo un'occhiata al nostro appartamento per assicurarci che sia in ordine.
dee-A-mo oon-ok-kee-A-ta al NOS-tro ap-par-ta-MEN-to per as-see-koo-RAR-chee keh SEE-a in OR-dee-neh.

THE LAST 24 HOURS BEFORE LEAVING

Where are the passports?
Dove sono i passaporti?
DO-veh SO-no ee pas-sa-POR-tee?

Did you fill out the customs forms?
Avete riempito i moduli degli* ospiti?
a-VEH-teh ree-em-PEE-to ee MO-doo-lee DEL-lee OS-pee-tee?

Make sure to pack everything.
Assicurati di mettere tutto in valigia.
as-see-KOO-ra-tee dee MET-teh-reh TOOT-to in va-LEE-jee-A.

Where are we going?
Dove stiamo andando?
DO-veh stee-A-mo an-DAN-do?

Which flight are we taking?
Che volo prendiamo?
keh VO-lo pren-dee-A-mo?

Check your pockets.
Controlla le tue tasche.
kon-TROL-la leh TOO-eh TAS-keh.

I need to declare some things for customs.
Devo dichiarare alcune cose che ho comprato.
DEH-vo dee-kee-a-RA-reh al-KOO-neh KO-seh keh o kom-PRA-to.

No, I have nothing to declare.
No, non ho nulla da dichiarare.
no, non o NOOL-la da dee-kee-a-RA-reh.

What is the checkout time?
A che ora si effettua il check out?
a keh O-ra see ef-FET-too-a eel check out?

177

Make sure your phone is charged.
Assicurati che il tuo cellulare sia carico.
as-see-KOO-ra-tee keh eel TOO-o chel-loo-LA-reh SEE-a KA-ree-ko.

Is there a fee attached to this?
C'è una tassa da pagare con questo?
CHEH OO-na TAS-sa da pa-GA-reh kon KWES-to?

Do we have any outstanding bills to pay?
Abbiamo delle spese in sospeso da pagare?
ab-bee-A-mo DEL-leh SPEH-seh so-SPEH-so da Pa-ga-reh?

What time does our flight leave?
A che ora parte il tuo volo?
a keh O-ra PAR-teh eel TOO-o VO-lo?

What time do we need to be in the airport?
A che ora dobbiamo essere in aeroporto?
a keh O-ra dob-bee-A-mo ES-seh-reh in a-eh-ro-POR-to?

How bad is the traffic going in the direction of the airport?
Com'è il traffico andando in direzione dell'aeroporto?
kom-EH eel TRAF-fee-ko an-DAN-do in dee-re-zee-O-neh dell-a-eh-ro-POR-to?

Are there any detours we can take?
Ci sono delle deviazioni da prendere?
chee SO-no DEL-leh deh-vee-a-zee-O-nee da PREN-deh-reh?

What haven't we seen from our list since we've been down here?
Cosa non abbiamo ancora visto della nostra lista da quando siamo qui?
KO-sa non ab-bee-A-mo an-KO-ra VIS-to DEL-la NOS-tra LIS-ta da KWAN-do see-A-mo KWEE?

We should really buy some souvenirs here.
Dovremmo proprio comprare dei souvenir qui.
do-VREM-mo PRO-pree-o kom-peh-RA-reh DEH-ee souvenir KWEE.

Do you know any shortcuts that will get us there faster?
Conosci qualche scorciatoia che ci possa far arrivare più in fretta?
ko-NO-shee KWAL-keh skor-chee-a-TO-ee-a keh chee POS-sa far ar-ree-VA-reh PEW in FRET-ta?

GPS the location and save it.
Localizza il luogo col GPS e salvalo.
lo-ka-LEEZ-za eel loo-O-go kol GPS eh SAL-va-lo.

Are the items we're bringing back allowed on the plane?
Le cose che stiamo portando sull'aereo sono permesse?
leh KO-seh keh stee-A-mo por-TAN-do sool-a-EH-reh-o SO-no per-MES-seh?

We should call our family back home before leaving.
Dovremmo chiamare la nostra famiglia* a casa prima di partire.
do-VREM-mo kee-a-MA-reh la NOS-tra fa-MEEL-lee-a a KA-sa PREE-ma dee par-TEE-reh.

Make sure the pet cage is locked.
Assicurati che il trasportino sia chiuso.
as-see-KOO-ra-tee keh eel tras-por-TEE-no SEE-a kee-OO-so.

Go through your luggage again.
Controlla di nuovo il bagaglio.
kon-TROL-la dee noo-O-vo eel ba-GAL-lee-o.

MORE FROM LINGO MASTERY

Do you know what the hardest thing for an Italian learner is?

Finding PROPER reading material that they can handle...which is precisely the reason we've written this book!

Teachers love giving out tough, expert-level literature to their students, books that present many new problems to the reader and force them to search for words in a dictionary every five minutes — it's not entertaining, useful or motivating for the student at all, and many soon give up on learning at all!

In this book we have compiled 20 easy-to-read, compelling and fun stories that will allow you to expand your vocabulary and give you the tools to improve your grasp of the wonderful Italian tongue.

How Italian Short Stories for Beginners works:

- Each story will involve an important lesson of the tools in the Italian language (Verbs, Adjectives, Past Tense, Giving Directions, and more), involving an interesting and entertaining story with realistic dialogues and day-to-day situations.

- The summaries follow a synopsis in Italian and in English of what you just read, both to review the lesson and for you to see if you understood what the tale was about.
- At the end of those summaries, you'll be provided with a list of the most relevant vocabulary involved in the lesson, as well as slang and sayings that you may not have understood at first glance!
- Finally, you'll be provided with a set of tricky questions in Italian, providing you with the chance to prove that you learned something in the story. Don't worry if you don't know the answer to any — we will provide them immediately after, but no cheating!

So look no further! Pick up your copy of **Italian Short Stories for Beginners** and start learning Italian right now!

Have you been trying to learn Italian, but feel that you're a long way off from talking like a native?

Do you want to have an efficient resource to teach you words and phrases very commonly used in endless scenarios?

Are you looking to learn Italian vocabulary quickly and effectively without being swarmed with complicated rules?

If you answered *"Yes!"* to at least one of the previous questions, then this book is definitely for you! We've created **Italian Vocabulary Builder - 2222 Italian Phrases To Learn Italian And Grow Your Vocabulary** – a powerful list of common Italian terms used in context that will vastly expand your vocabulary and boost your fluency in the "language of music", as it is romantically called.

In this book you will find:

- A detailed introduction with a brief, descriptive guide on how to improve your learning
- A list of **2222** keywords in common phrases in Italian and their translations.
- Finally, a conclusion to close the lesson and ensure you've made good use of the material

But we haven't even told you what we've got in store for you, have we? In this book, you will find phrases relevant to the most common and essential subjects, such as: Adjectives, Animals, Entertainment, Family and Friendship, Grammar, Health, Jobs Time, Synonyms and dozens of other must-know topics.

So what are you waiting for? Open the pages of **Italian Vocabulary Builder - 2222 Italian Phrases To Learn Italian And Grow Your Vocabulary** and start boosting your language skills today!

Is conversational Italian learning a little too tricky for you? Do you have no idea how to order a meal or book a room at a hotel?

If your answer to any of the previous questions was 'Yes', then this book is for you!

If there's ever been something tougher than learning the grammar rules of a new language, it's finding the way to speak with other people in that tongue. Any student knows this – we can try our best at practicing, but you always want to avoid making embarrassing mistakes or not getting your message through correctly.

"How do I get out of this situation?" many students ask themselves, to no avail, but no answer is forthcoming.

Until now.

We have compiled **MORE THAN ONE HUNDRED** conversational Italian dialogues for beginners along with their translations, allowing new Italian speakers to have the necessary tools to begin studying how to set a meeting, rent a car or tell a doctor that they don't feel well. We're not wasting time here with conversations that don't go anywhere: if you want to know how to solve problems (while learning a ton of Italian along the way, obviously), this book is for you!

184

How Conversational Italian Dialogues works:

- Each new chapter will have a fresh, new story between two people who wish to solve a common, day-to-day issue that you will surely encounter in real life.
- An Italian version of the conversation will take place first, followed by an English translation. This ensures that you fully understood just what it was that they were saying.
- Before and after the main section of the book, we shall provide you with an introduction and conclusion that will offer you important strategies, tips and tricks to allow you to get the absolute most out of this learning material.
- That's about it! Simple, useful and incredibly helpful; you will NOT need another conversational Italian book once you have begun reading and studying this one!

We want you to feel comfortable while learning the tongue; after all, no language should be a barrier for you to travel around the world and expand your social circles!

So look no further! Pick up your copy of Conversational Italian Dialogues and start learning Italian right now!

CONCLUSION

Congratulations! You have reached the end of this book and learned over **1,500** ways to express yourself in the Italian language! It is a moment to celebrate, since you are now much closer to achieving complete fluency of the Italian tongue.

However, the learning simply cannot end here – you may have unlocked a massive amount of incredibly useful day-to-day phrases that will get you anywhere you need to go, but are you prepared to use them correctly? Furthermore, will you actually remember them during your travels when faced with one of the situations we've presented in this book?

Only by continuously studying the material found in previous chapters will you ever be able to summon the words and phrases encountered above, since it isn't a matter of *what* the phrases are, but *how* and *when* to use them. Knowing the exact context is crucial, as well as reinforcing your knowledge with other materials.

For this reason, we have created a quick list of tips to make the most of this Italian Phrasebook and expanding your vocabulary and grasp of the Italian language:

1. **Practice every day:** You can be very good at something thanks to the gift of natural talent, but practice is the only way to *stay* good. Make sure to constantly pick up the book and read the words, saying them out loud and taking note of your mistakes so you can correct them.

2. **Read while listening:** A very popular and modern way of learning a new language is by using the RwL (reading while listening) method. It has proven that this method can greatly boost fluency, help you ace language tests and improve your learning in other subjects. Feel free to try out our audiobooks and other listening materials in Italian – you'll love them!

3. **Studying in groups:** It's always best to go on an adventure together – even if it's a language adventure! You'll enjoy yourself

more if you can find someone who wants to learn with you. Look to friends, your partner, your family members or colleagues for support, and maybe they can even help you make the process easier and quicker!

4. **Creating your own exercises:** This book provides you with plenty of material for your learning processes, and you will probably be happy with reading it every time you can... however, you need to increase the difficulty by looking for other words and phrases in the Italian language which you don't know the pronunciation to, and trying to decipher it for yourself. Use the knowledge you've gained with previous lessons and discover entirely new words!

With that said, we have now fully concluded this Italian Phrasebook which will surely accelerate your learning to new levels. Don't forget to follow every tip we've included, and to keep an eye out for our additional Italian materials.

Made in United States
North Haven, CT
13 January 2022

14760789R00107